CONTEMPORARY'S
LOOK AT THE U·S·
BOOK 2

CAROLE CROSS

ESL Coordinator
El Monte-Rosemead Adult School
El Monte, California

with

ROB PARAL

Research Associate
NALEO (National Association of
Latino Elected and Appointed Officials)
Washington, D.C.

Project Coordinator
Julie Landau

Editor
Betsy Rubin

CB

CONTEMPORARY
BOOKS

CHICAGO · NEW YORK

Library of Congress Cataloging-in-Publication Data

Cross, Carole.
    Look at the U.S. : book 2 / Carole Cross.
       p.   cm. — (An ESL/civics series)
    Cover title: Contemporary's look at the U.S.
    "Based on the federal citizenship texts."
    ISBN 0-8092-4386-5
    1. Civics.   I. Title.   II. Title: Look at the US.   III. Title:
Contemporary's look at the U.S.   IV. Series.
JK1758.C763   1989
320.473—dc19   88-37057
                                         CIP

Photo credits
Page 1: The Bettmann Archive. Page 3: H. S. Rice. Courtesy, Department of Library Services, American Museum of Natural History (Negative 312686). Pages 7 and 11: The Bettmann Archive. Pages 15 and 17: Culver Pictures. Pages 19, 23, and 25: The Bettmann Archive. Page 29: Culver Pictures. Pages 37 and 41: The Bettmann Archive. Page 45: Culver Pictures. Page 49: The Bettmann Archive. Page 51: AP/Wide World Photos. Page 55: UPI/Bettmann Newsphotos. Page 57: © George Bellerose/Stock Boston. Page 59: © Daniel S. Brody/Stock Boston. Page 65: UPI/Bettmann Newsphotos. Page 69: © Owen Franken/Stock Boston. Pages 71, 73, and 77: AP/Wide World Photos. Page 79: UPI/Bettmann Newsphotos. Page 83: AP/Wide World Photos. Page 87: Culver Pictures. Page 91: © Burt Glinn/Magnum Photos.

Published by Contemporary Books, Inc.
180 North Michigan Avenue, Chicago, Illinois 60601
Manufactured in the United States of America
International Standard Book Number: 0-8092-4386-5

Published simultaneously in Canada by
Beaverbooks, Ltd.
195 Allstate Parkway
Valleywood Business Park
Markham, Ontario L3R 4T8
Canada

Editorial Director	*Cover Design*
Caren Van Slyke	Lois Koehler
Editorial	*Illustrator*
Kathy Osmus	Rosemary Morrissey-Herzberg
Craig Bolt	
Lisa Dillman	*Photo Researcher*
Susan Grzyb	Julie Laffin
Editorial/Production Manager	*Art & Production*
Patricia Reid	Princess Louise El
	Jan Geist
Production Editor	
Craig Bolt	*Typography*
	Carol Schoder

Cover photo © The Image Bank
Photographer: David W. Hamilton

Contents

To the Instructor

The *Look at the U.S.* series was specially designed to help ESL teachers introduce civics concepts into the classroom. This multi-level series introduces the fundamentals of U.S. history and government and is based on the federal citizenship textbooks. This flexible series can serve as texts for:

- special ESL/civics classes for amnesty students
- citizenship classes
- standard ESL classes

In addition to this book, *Look at the U.S., Book 1*, the series includes:

- *Look at the U.S., Book 2*
- *Teacher's Guide, Books 1 & 2*
- *Look at the U.S., Literacy Level*
- *Teacher's Guide, Literacy Level*

Instructional Design for This Book

The purpose of this book is to teach the basics of U.S. history and government by reinforcing the English language skills of listening, speaking, reading, and writing. To accomplish this, each lesson incorporates the features shown on the chart below.

Books 1 & 2—Lesson Design

FEATURE *(per lesson)*	SKILL	SOURCE
Setting the Stage	listening and speaking	teacher's guide
Before You Read	listening, speaking, and pre-reading	student text
Reading Passage	reading	student text
After You Read	reading comprehension	student text
Think About . . .	speaking, listening, or writing	student text
Using New Words	vocabulary development	student text
Sentence Completion (*Book 1*)	writing	student text
Express Your Ideas (*Book 2*)	writing	student text

These optional activities can be presented at the teacher's discretion:		
Listening Activity	listening and speaking	teacher's guide
Group Activity	listening and speaking	teacher's guide
Writing Activity	writing	teacher's guide

Activities found in the teacher's guide should be used to supplement the text and, most importantly, to actively draw the students into the learning process.

Teacher's Guide for Books 1 and 2

The teacher's guide for Books 1 and 2 provides:

- an overview of the key components of each lesson
- chapter-by-chapter ideas for supplementary classroom activities
- handouts to use in the classroom

Throughout your work with this series, you will be given the opportunity to link important issues in American government and history to concerns facing your students in their daily lives. In particular, teacher's guide activities will help you relate civics topics to everyday life.

The Multi-Level Approach

Books 1 and 2 address the same key concepts in U.S. history and government. However, since students have varying degrees of proficiency in English, the books are written at different levels. Book 1 is aimed at students who can speak, read, and write some basic English and who have had some education in their own country. Book 2 assumes a higher educational level and greater fluency in English.

Book 1 may be too difficult for some of the beginning-level students. For this reason, there is a literacy-level book (and accompanying teacher's guide) in the *Look at the U.S.* series.

For more information on other books in this series, contact:

Contemporary Books
Adult Education Division
180 North Michigan Avenue
Chicago, Illinois 60601

Our toll-free number is 1-800-621-1918.

For more information on how to use this book and for additional classroom activities, see *Look at the U.S. Teacher's Guide—Books 1 & 2.*

U.S. History

New arrivals to the U.S. in the 1800s.

Chapter 1
Native Americans

Many Native Americans lived in villages.

BEFORE YOU READ

1. The Indian people are also called Native Americans. What does "native" mean?

2. What is your native country?

3. Who are the people in the picture? What are they doing?

4. Who lived in North America first—the Native Americans or the Europeans?

5. Do Native Americans still live in the United States? Where?

3

Native Americans

The first people to live in North America came from Asia. Look at the map on page 5. This map shows that at one time there was a piece of land connecting Alaska and Siberia, a part of Asia. This land, called a land bridge, appeared when the level of the ocean was very low.

People looking for animals to hunt left Asia and entered North America. These people continued to move south and east. They came to North America from Asia over many thousands of years.

These first inhabitants of the Americas moved to all parts of North and South America. As groups adapted themselves to different regions, they developed their own cultures, along with more than 1,500 languages. Several groups developed into powerful and advanced societies.

The Native Americans used many products that were later adopted by countries in all parts of the world. Corn, potatoes, tomatoes, tobacco, and chocolate are just a few of the products that were first used by Native Americans.

The arrival of European colonists in the Americas caused a tragic conflict. The Europeans dominated and abused the Native Americans. They fought with them and took away their land. Many Native Americans were forced to live on special areas of land called reservations.

The Native Americans lived in every part of the Americas, and their cultures were rich and diverse. Modern society has received many benefits from the contributions of these first Americans.

AFTER YOU READ

Choose the best answer to complete the sentence.

1. The first inhabitants of North America came from

   a. South America
   b. Europe
   c. Asia
   d. Central America

3. The native people of the Americas

   a. did not adapt to North America
   b. returned to Asia
   c. did not develop powerful societies
   d. developed more than 1,500 languages

2. Corn, potatoes, and tomatoes were

   a. brought to the Americas by the Europeans
   b. first grown in the Americas
   c. not used by the Native Americans
   d. only used in North America

4. The European colonists

   a. spoke more than 1,500 languages
   b. came to the Americas from Siberia
   c. abused the Native Americans
   d. lived on reservations

4

USING NEW WORDS

Choose from the words below to complete the sentences.

contributions   reservation   cultures   inhabitants

tobacco   conflict   abused

1. The first _____ of North America came from Asia.

2. The Native Americans developed a wide variety of _____

   and languages.

3. A tragic _____ developed between the Europeans and

   the Native Americans.

4. The European colonists _____ the Native Americans.

5. Native Americans have made many _____ to modern

   society, such as art and different crops.

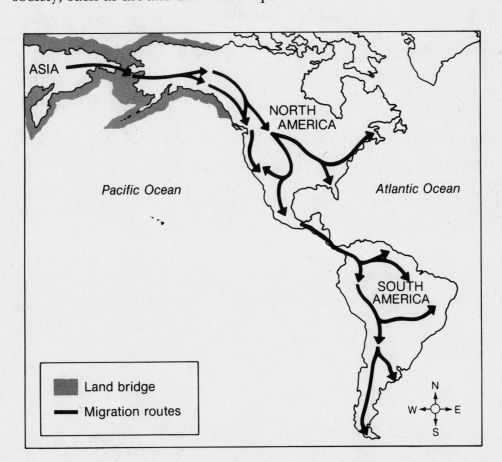

Thousands of years ago, people crossed a small piece of land to come from Asia to North America.

THINK ABOUT THE NATIVE AMERICANS

Answer the following questions.

1. Where did the Native Americans come from?

2. How did the Native Americans come to North America?

3. In what parts of the Americas did the Native Americans live?

4. Why do you think the people of North and South America spoke many languages?

5. Why do you think the Europeans could dominate the Native Americans?

Answers for this chapter start on page 108.

EXPRESS YOUR IDEAS

Think about the Native Americans before the Europeans came and after the Europeans came. How do you think the Europeans changed the lives of the Native Americans?

Answers will vary.

Chapter 2
Christopher Columbus and the New World

Christopher Columbus claimed the New World for the Queen of Spain.

BEFORE YOU READ

1. Why did you come to the United States?

2. Why do people travel to new countries?

3. How did Columbus travel to the New World?

4. In what other ways did people travel at the time of Columbus?

5. What do you think Columbus was looking for when he crossed the ocean?

Christopher Columbus

At the time of Columbus, in the 1400s, people from Europe often traded products with people in Asia. Europeans traveled to Asia to buy valuable goods such as silk and spices. To reach Asia, Europeans had to travel by land, and the trip was difficult and dangerous.

Christopher Columbus was an Italian navigator who believed that there was an easier way to reach Asia from Europe. Columbus believed that he could reach Asia by sailing west across the Atlantic Ocean. He convinced the Queen of Spain to help him, and she gave Columbus three sailing ships: the *Niña*, the *Pinta*, and the *Santa María*. She also provided men to sail with him.

In the 1400s, most people believed that the earth was flat. They thought that if a person sailed too far across the ocean he would fall off the end of the earth. So they thought Columbus was crazy.

In the year 1492, Columbus crossed the Atlantic Ocean to look for a new route to Asia. After about 30 days of travel, he and his men reached land. They believed that they were near India, in Asia, so they called the people they met "Indians." Of course, Columbus was not in Asia. He had reached the New World: North America and South America.

There were two important results of this trip. People learned that the earth was round, not flat. Also, Europeans began to colonize the New World.

AFTER YOU READ

Choose the best answer to complete the sentence.

1. Columbus wanted
   a. to find the New World
   b. to sail to Italy
   c. to travel by land
   d. to sail to Asia

2. At the time of Columbus, many Europeans
   a. traveled by ship to Asia
   b. believed the earth was flat
   c. sailed with Columbus to the New World
   d. sold silk and spices in Asia

3. Europeans went to Asia

    a. in the *Niña*, the *Pinta*, and the *Santa María*
    b. to prove the earth was flat
    c. to buy goods
    d. to discover the New World

4. After the trip by Columbus,

    a. people knew the earth was flat
    b. the Europeans colonized the New World
    c. people stopped buying silk and spices
    d. the Asians colonized the New World

USING NEW WORDS

Use words from the reading passage to fill in the blanks.

Example: Europeans bought these things in Asia: ____silk____ and

____spices____ (*paragraph 1*)

Europeans traveled to Asia to buy valuable goods such as **silk** and **spices**.

1. A person who directs a sailing ship: _____ (*paragraph 2*)

2. The opposite of round: _____ (*paragraph 5*)

3. To create communities in a new place: to _____

(*paragraph 5*)

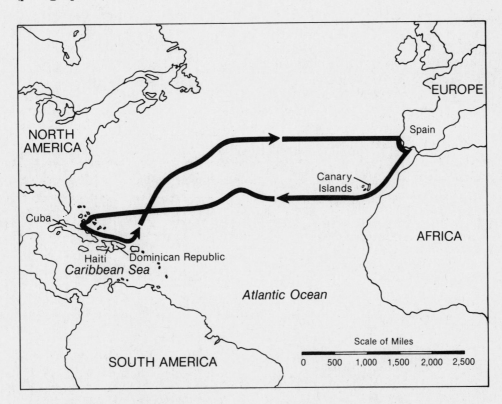

This map shows how Columbus traveled to the New World and back to Spain.

9

THINK ABOUT COLUMBUS

Answer the following questions.

1. At the time of Columbus, how did Europeans travel to Asia?

2. Why did Columbus sail across the ocean?

3. Why do you think Columbus asked the Queen of Spain for help?

4. Why did Columbus think he was near India?

5. How did Columbus change history?

Answers for this chapter start on page 108.

EXPRESS YOUR IDEAS

After Columbus made his trip, the Europeans began to colonize the New World. Do you think the world is better or worse because of what Columbus did?

Answers will vary.

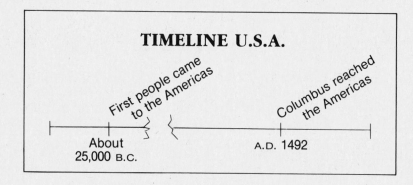

TIMELINE U.S.A.

Chapter 3
Jamestown and Plymouth

Native Americans and settlers eating the first Thanksgiving dinner.

BEFORE YOU READ

1. What was your first year in the United States like?

2. Is it difficult to start a new life in a new land? Why?

3. What is a colony?

4. Why did people come to the early colonies in the New World?

5. Why was life in the early colonies difficult?

Jamestown and Plymouth

About 100 years after Columbus reached the New World, England began to send people to build communities in North America. These communities were called colonies. The first permanent English colony was called Jamestown.

In 1607, 105 settlers left England to create the colony at Jamestown, in what is now the state of Virginia. At Jamestown the settlers made contact with the Native Americans, whom they called "Indians." The settlers began to grow tobacco and other crops and hunted wild animals, such as deer and turkey, for meat.

John Smith was a strong leader of the people in Jamestown. He forced men to work and helped them build homes for themselves and their families.

In 1620 another group of colonists, the Pilgrims, left England for the New World. The Pilgrims came to North America because they could not practice their own religion in Europe. They sailed in a ship called the *Mayflower*, and they created the colony of Plymouth in what is now the state of Massachusetts.

The Pilgrims suffered from sickness and lack of food at Plymouth. During their first 18 months, nearly half of the colonists died. But the Native Americans taught the Pilgrims much about the plants and animals of the New World. Because of the Indians' help, the Pilgrims finally had a good harvest of crops.

To celebrate the good harvest, the Pilgrims prepared a large meal which they shared with the Indians. This feast is now a holiday called Thanksgiving Day, and it is celebrated on the fourth Thursday in November.

Today, people in the United States often have large reunions on Thanksgiving. Families gather to talk and eat lots of food like turkey, sweet potatoes, and cranberries.

AFTER YOU READ

Choose the best answer to complete the sentence.

1. The Pilgrims lived
   a. at Jamestown
   b. in what is now the state of Virginia
   c. at Plymouth
   d. in the first English colony

2. People came from England to North America
   a. to sail to Asia
   b. to hunt wild animals
   c. to build communities
   d. to have big meals

3. At Jamestown, the colonists

    a. grew tobacco and other crops

    b. could not practice their religion

    c. sailed on the *Mayflower*

    d. celebrated the first Thanksgiving

4. The Pilgrims had a big meal

    a. to celebrate a good harvest

    b. to celebrate their return to England

    c. to learn about plants and animals

    d. before a successful harvest

USING NEW WORDS

Choose from the words below to complete the sentences.

    reunions   colonies   suffered   meal   families   harvest

1. People left Europe to create _____ in North America.

2. At Plymouth, the Pilgrims _____ from sickness.

3. With help from the Indians, the Pilgrims had a good _____.

4. After the first harvest, the Pilgrims celebrated with a great _____.

5. Families often have large get-togethers called _____

on Thanksgiving Day.

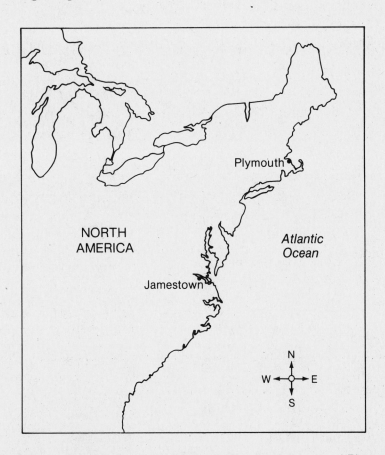

This map of the eastern United States shows Jamestown and Plymouth.

THINK ABOUT JAMESTOWN AND PLYMOUTH

Answer the following questions.

1. Why is the colony at Jamestown important in history?
2. What kind of difficulties did the Pilgrims have in their first year at Plymouth?
3. Why did the Pilgrims celebrate with a big meal?
4. Why is Thanksgiving Day an important holiday in the United States today?
5. Why do you think some Europeans wanted to live in the colonies?

Answers for this chapter start on page 108.

EXPRESS YOUR IDEAS

The first colonists needed many skills and abilities to survive. What types of skills were needed to survive in the New World?

Answers will vary.

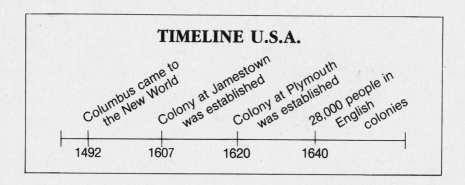

Chapter 4
Beginnings of the Revolution

Angry colonists threw tea into Boston Harbor to protest a tax on tea.

BEFORE YOU READ

1. What is a colony?

2. Think about history. Which countries in the world have had colonies? Was your native country ever a colony?

3. Why do nations want to have colonies?

4. What is a tax?

5. What do you pay taxes for? Do you like to pay taxes?

Rebellion in the Colonies

By the 1700s, there were English colonies up and down most of the east coast of North America. England controlled these colonies. The colonies paid taxes to the English government, and there were English soldiers in the colonies.

The population of the colonies grew, and so did their economic strength. As the colonies became stronger, they began to want greater independence and fairness from England. Two incidents showed that the colonies were serious about wanting greater independence.

In Boston in 1770, a group of colonists protested in front of the Customs House, a place where certain taxes were paid. The colonists yelled at an English soldier and then at other soldiers that arrived at the Customs House.

Some colonists threw snowballs at the soldiers. The crowd grew more and more restless, and the soldiers became angry. In the confusion, the English soldiers fired their weapons at the unarmed colonists.

Five colonists were killed by the gunfire. The first person killed was a black man, Crispus Attucks. The deaths of the colonists became known as the Boston Massacre.

Three years later, in 1773, colonists in Boston protested against a tax that the English had put on tea. A group of 60 colonists dressed themselves as Indians and went on an English ship in Boston Harbor. They threw many boxes of valuable tea into the ocean.

The action in Boston Harbor was called the Boston Tea Party, and it greatly angered the English government. The Boston Tea Party showed that the colonists were not afraid to challenge the English government.

AFTER YOU READ

Choose the best answer to complete the sentence.

1. In the 1700s, the colonies
   a. became stronger
   b. did not want more independence
   c. were on the west coast of North America
   d. were losing population

2. In the Boston Massacre, English soldiers
   a. wanted independence for the colonies
   b. threw tea in Boston Harbor
   c. fired weapons at colonists
   d. dressed themselves as Indians

3. During the Boston Tea Party, colonists protested about

   a. the Boston Massacre
   b. the poor quality of tea
   c. Boston Harbor
   d. a tax on tea

4. Sixty colonists dressed themselves as Indians

   a. to fire at English soldiers
   b. to look like English soldiers
   c. and paid taxes to England
   d. and threw tea into Boston Harbor

USING NEW WORDS

Use words from the reading passage to fill in the blanks. Follow the example on page 9.

Example: The communities created by the English in the New

World: __colonies__ (*paragraph 1*)

1. Money paid to a government: _____ (*paragraph 1*)

2. People who fight for a country: _____ (*paragraph 1*)

3. Power: _____ (*paragraph 2*)

4. People who created the colonies: _____ (*paragraph 3*)

5. Guns and knives: _____ (*paragraph 4*)

6. Without weapons: _____ (*paragraph 4*)

In the Boston Massacre, English soldiers shot and killed American colonists.

THINK ABOUT REBELLION IN THE COLONIES

Answer the following questions.

1. Why did the colonies want more independence from England?
2. How did the Boston Massacre begin?
3. In the Boston Tea Party, why do you think the colonists dressed like Indians?
4. Why do you think the English government was angry about the Boston Tea Party?
5. Why were the Boston Massacre and the Boston Tea Party important in U.S. history?

Answers for this chapter start on page 109.

EXPRESS YOUR IDEAS

Think of the way that the colonies grew stronger. Why do you think they wanted independence?

Answers will vary.

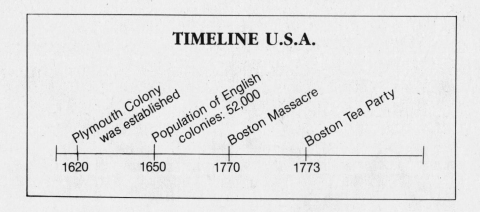

TIMELINE U.S.A.

Plymouth Colony was established — 1620

Population of English colonies: 52,000 — 1650

Boston Massacre — 1770

Boston Tea Party — 1773

Chapter 5
The Declaration of Independence

A representative signs the Declaration of Independence.

BEFORE YOU READ

1. What makes a person independent?

2. What makes a country independent?

3. How did the American colonists feel about the English government?

4. Does your country have a national holiday? What does it celebrate?

5. On what day do Americans celebrate their independence?

The Independence of the Colonies

As you read in the last chapter, the American colonies began to rebel against the English government. At the same time, the colonies began to develop their own system of government. In 1774, representatives of 12 of the 13 colonies went to the city of Philadelphia. Together, they created the Continental Congress, a new form of government for the colonies.

At first, the Continental Congress demanded only that England recognize certain basic rights of the colonies. As time passed, however, more members of the Congress began to demand complete independence from England.

In 1776, the Continental Congress decided to write a formal explanation of why the colonies wanted to be independent. This document is the Declaration of Independence.

Thomas Jefferson, who later became the third U.S. president, wrote most of the Declaration of Independence. The Declaration announced to the world that the colonies were "Free and Independent States" that would no longer be controlled by the English government.

The Declaration is also a defense of the rights of people. It proclaims that "all men are created equal" and that people have the right to "life, liberty, and the pursuit of happiness." According to the Declaration, governments cannot take these rights away from people.

The Continental Congress approved the Declaration of Independence on July 4, 1776. Eventually, representatives from all 13 colonies signed the Declaration. This showed the English government that the colonies were united in their desire for independence.

On July 4, 1776, the United States of America became an independent nation. Each year, the "Fourth of July," or "Independence Day," is celebrated as our nation's birthday.

AFTER YOU READ

Choose the best answer to complete the sentence.

1. The Declaration of Independence
   a. gave independence to the English
   b. was approved on July 4, 1774
   c. was written by George Washington
   d. declared the independence of the colonies

2. The colonists wanted
   a. to control the English
   b. to control themselves
   c. to have a national birthday
   d. to be more dependent on England

3. The Declaration of Independence says that

    a. the Fourth of July is the nation's birthday

    b. Thomas Jefferson was a president

    c. the government can take away people's rights

    d. people have certain rights

4. The Fourth of July is celebrated

    a. only in Philadelphia

    b. as the nation's birthday

    c. to remember Thomas Jefferson

    d. in the U.S. and England

USING NEW WORDS

Choose from the words below to complete the sentences.

birthday   happiness   independence   approving
explanation   proclaimed

1. The colonies wanted to control themselves. They wanted

_____ from England.

2. The colonies showed England that they wanted more rights

by _____ the Declaration of Independence.

3. The rights of people are _____ by the Declaration of

Independence.

4. The day that the Declaration of Independence was approved is known

as the _____ of the United States.

These 13 colonies declared their independence from England in 1776.

THINK ABOUT THE DECLARATION OF INDEPENDENCE

Answer the following questions.

1. Why did some colonists write the Declaration of Independence?

2. Why did the colonists want to be independent from England?

3. What happened on July 4, 1776?

4. Why was it important that representatives of all the colonies signed the Declaration of Independence?

5. What do you think the King of England thought about the Declaration of Independence?

Answers for this chapter start on page 109.

EXPRESS YOUR IDEAS

How is Independence Day celebrated in the United States? Does your native country celebrate an independence day? If so, describe how.

Answers will vary.

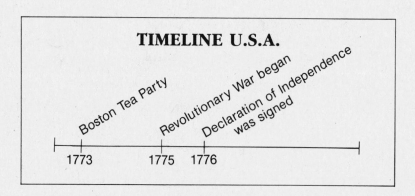

TIMELINE U.S.A.

Boston Tea Party

Revolutionary War began

Declaration of Independence was signed

1773   1775 1776

Chapter 6
George Washington and the Revolution

George Washington and his men fought many battles.

BEFORE YOU READ

1. Who were some important early leaders of your native country?

2. What is a revolutionary war?

3. Has your native country ever had a revolutionary war?

4. Why do revolutions happen?

5. Why is George Washington famous?

Revolution and the Nation's First Leader

The American Revolutionary War began in April 1775. In that month, English soldiers marched from Boston to the town of Concord, Massachusetts. They wanted to destroy the guns and ammunition that the colonists kept in Concord.

As the English passed the town of Lexington, however, a group of colonists fired weapons at them. The colonists were prepared to fight because they knew that the English were coming. A man named Paul Revere and his companions had ridden their horses through the night from Boston to tell the colonists that the English were coming.

From Lexington, the English moved on to Concord. At Concord about 350 colonists attacked the English. As the English soldiers returned to Boston, thousands of colonists fired at them. The Revolutionary War had begun.

George Washington was the commander of the colonial army, known as the Continental Army, in many battles during the Revolutionary War. Washington is famous for a surprise attack that he led at Trenton on Christmas night.

In the Battle of Trenton, Washington and his soldiers crossed a river during a stormy Christmas night. He and the colonists were able to surprise and capture 900 enemy soldiers. The enemy soldiers were not prepared to fight. When they saw Washington and his men, they gave up their guns.

In 1781, Washington led the Continental Army in the Battle of Yorktown. In this last battle of the American Revolution, more than 7,000 English soldiers surrendered. The war ended in 1783, but this battle broke the spirit of the English. In 1789, George Washington became the first president of the United States. Today, he is known as "The Father of His Country."

AFTER YOU READ

Choose the best answer to complete the sentence.

1. The American colonial army
   a. lost the Revolutionary War
   b. lost a battle at Trenton
   c. was attacked by colonists at Lexington
   d. was called the Continental Army

2. George Washington was
   a. the first president
   b. born in 1775
   c. the leader of the English army
   d. attacked at Trenton

3. At Lexington,

    a. the colonists fired on English soldiers

    b. the Revolutionary War ended

    c. 900 English soldiers were killed

    d. the English destroyed guns

4. The last battle of the American Revolution was at

    a. Lexington

    b. Concord

    c. Yorktown

    d. Trenton

USING NEW WORDS

Use words from the reading passage to fill in the blanks. Follow the example on page 9.

Example: The leader of an army: <u>commander</u> (*paragraph 4*)

1. Members of an army: _____ (*paragraph 1*)

2. The army or country that you fight against:

_____ (*paragraph 5*)

3. Gave up: _____ (*paragraph 6*)

4. The leader of the American government: _____ (*paragraph 6*)

An English leader falls, and the English lose the Battle of Yorktown.

THINK ABOUT THE AMERICAN REVOLUTION

Answer the following questions.

1. When did the Revolutionary War begin and end?

2. Why were the colonists at Lexington ready for the English?

3. What was the result of the Revolutionary War?

4. Why did the colonists have to fight a war for independence?

5. Why do you think George Washington is famous?

Answers for this chapter start on page 110.

EXPRESS YOUR IDEAS

The American colonists won the Revolutionary War. Why do you think they were able to defeat the English, who were much more powerful?

Answers will vary.

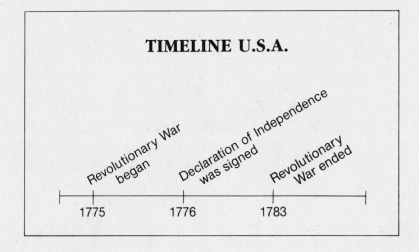

Chapter Review 1

WORD FIND

All of the words in the list are hidden in the box. They go from left to right and from top to bottom. Circle each one. One is done for you.

W	A	R	U	C	F	T	H	M
A	R	M	Y	O	B	P	O	Z
S	E	T	T	L	E	R	L	V
O	L	A	N	O	V	O	I	I
L	I	X	Q	N	P	T	D	L
D	G	S	X	Y	S	E	A	L
I	I	G	O	O	D	S	Y	A
E	O	R	I	G	H	T	S	G
R	N	S	H	I	P	V	W	E

✔ VILLAGE
SETTLER
COLONY
SHIP
RELIGION
SOLDIER
TAX
PROTEST
RIGHTS
HOLIDAYS
GOODS
ARMY
WAR

TIMELINE

Write the events in the correct order on the timeline. One of them is done for you.

~~Boston Tea Party~~
Columbus came to the Americas
Declaration of Independence
Plymouth colony was established

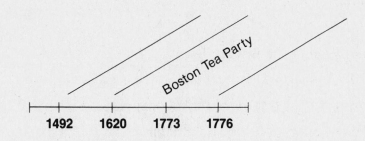

Boston Tea Party

1492   1620   1773   1776

MAP ACTIVITY

Label the original 13 colonies on this map. Use the arrows to the colonies that are too small to write on. Look back at page 21 if you need help.

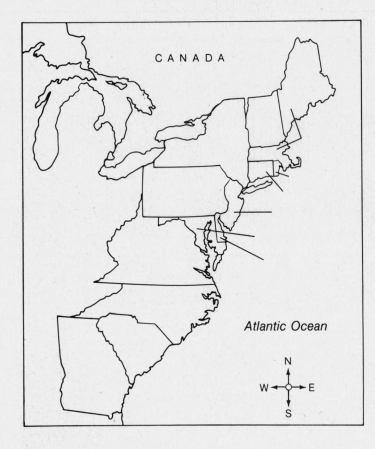

1. Connecticut
2. Delaware
3. Georgia
4. Maryland
5. Massachusetts
6. New Hampshire
7. New Jersey
8. New York
9. North Carolina
10. Pennsylvania
11. Rhode Island
12. South Carolina
13. Virginia

QUIZ

Find a partner and practice answering these questions.

1. Who was Christopher Columbus?

2. What were the first two English settlements?

3. Who were the Pilgrims?

4. What happened at the Boston Tea Party?

5. In 1776, how many English colonies were there?

6. Who wrote the Declaration of Independence?

7. What is the birthday of the United States?

8. Name the war in which the U.S. won independence from England.

9. Who was the great leader of this war?

10. Who was the first president of the United States?

Answers for this chapter review start on page 110.

Chapter 7
The Birth of the Constitution

The U.S. Constitution was approved at the Constitutional Convention.

BEFORE YOU READ

1. Think about your native country. Is it divided into states, provinces, or other regions?

2. What is a federal, or national, government?

3. What is a state government?

4. What is a law? Give some examples of laws in your city or state in the United States.

5. What is a constitution? Does every country have one?

The Beginning of the U.S. Government

As the 13 colonies became independent, they had to decide on what kind of government they needed. In 1781, the Continental Congress created the Articles of Confederation, a collection of laws that governed the states.

Unfortunately, the Articles of Confederation were not a satisfactory form of government. The individual states had too much power, and the national, or federal, government was too weak. For instance, under the Articles of Confederation, the federal government could not require the states to pay taxes.

The members of the Continental Congress, who represented the 13 new states, decided to replace the Articles of Confederation. In 1787, they met in Philadelphia to decide on the form of the new government. George Washington was the head of this meeting. The meeting, called the Constitutional Convention, resulted in the Constitution of the United States.

The Constitution carefully describes the structure of American government. For example, it created the system of courts and the position of the president. The Constitution contains the most important laws of the United States.

After the Constitution was written, the 13 states had to approve it. Each state discussed the Constitution and, by 1789, representatives from every state signed it.

By signing the Constitution, each state was saying that it would always obey the laws of the Constitution. In this way, the 13 individual states became the United States of America.

AFTER YOU READ

Choose the best answer to complete the sentence.

1. The Articles of Confederation
   a. functioned very well
   b. are still used today
   c. were written by Thomas Jefferson
   d. had serious problems

2. The Continental Congress
   a. replaced the Articles of Confederation
   b. still exists today
   c. defended the English government
   d. was created in 1871

3. The Constitution
   a. was approved by the English
   b. was created in 1779
   c. describes the U.S. government
   d. was never adopted

4. George Washington
   a. wrote the Articles of Confederation
   b. wrote the Constitution
   c. headed the Constitutional Convention
   d. forced the colonies to pay taxes

USING NEW WORDS

Use words from the reading passage to fill in the blanks. Follow the example on page 9.

Example: Made: ___*created*___ (*paragraph 1*)

1. Acceptable; good: _____ (*paragraph 2*)

2. The opposite of strong: _____ (*paragraph 2*)

3. To make someone do something: to _____ (*paragraph 2*)

4. Rules: _____ (*paragraph 4*)

5. Form; shape: _____ (*paragraph 4*)

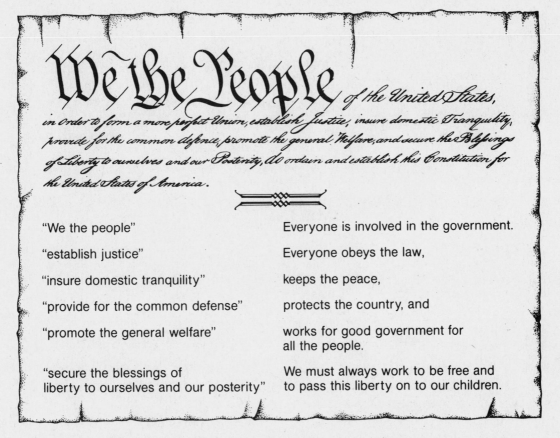

"We the people"	Everyone is involved in the government.
"establish justice"	Everyone obeys the law,
"insure domestic tranquility"	keeps the peace,
"provide for the common defense"	protects the country, and
"promote the general welfare"	works for good government for all the people.
"secure the blessings of liberty to ourselves and our posterity"	We must always work to be free and to pass this liberty on to our children.

The Preamble, or introduction, to the Constitution has these important ideas.

THINK ABOUT THE CONTINENTAL CONGRESS AND THE CONSTITUTION

Answer the following questions.

1. What was an important problem with the Articles of Confederation?

2. What replaced the Articles of Confederation?

3. Why was it necessary to create the Articles of Confederation and the Constitution?

4. Why was it important that every state approved the Constitution?

5. Why is the Constitution an important document?

Answers for this chapter start on page 111.

EXPRESS YOUR IDEAS

Before the Constitution was written, some states wanted to become separate, independent nations. Do you think it is good that the states became united? Why?

Answers will vary.

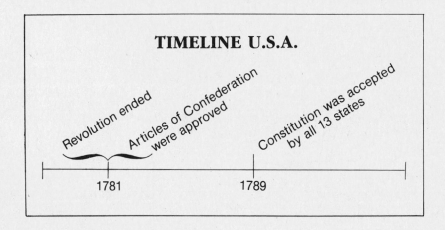

Chapter 8
The American Flag

The American flag has 50 stars for the 50 states.

BEFORE YOU READ

1. Describe the flag of your native country.

2. What are the colors of the flag of the United States?

3. How many stars are on the flag of the United States?

4. Where do you often see the American flag?

5. What are flags used for?

The Flag and the Pledge of Allegiance

The flag of the United States of America was originally created in 1777. Over the years, the number of stars on the flag has increased; this represents the growth of the United States.

However, the colors of the flag have never changed. The stars are white, the area behind the stars is blue, and the stripes are red and white.

Look at the picture of a flag on page 33. Notice that the flag has 13 stripes. Think about the early history of the United States. What does the number 13 remind you of?

The 13 stripes on the flag represent the 13 original colonies of the United States. Now look at the stars on the flag. There are 50 stars, and these stars represent the 50 states in the United States. Because of the stars and stripes on the flag, the flag is often called the "Stars and Stripes."

The number of stars on the flag has always equaled the number of states in the country. The first flag had only 13 stars, to represent the 13 colonies. In 1818, there were 20 states, and so the flag had 20 stars. The number of stars has increased to the 50 stars on the modern flag.

The flag is an important symbol of the United States. One way to show respect for the flag is to say the "Pledge of Allegiance." When a person says the "Pledge of Allegiance," he puts his right hand over his heart and says:

> I pledge allegiance to the flag of the United States of America, and to the republic for which it stands, one nation, under God, indivisible, with liberty and justice for all.

AFTER YOU READ

Choose the best answer to complete the sentence.

1. Today, the stars on the American flag
   a. represent the 13 original colonies
   b. represent the 50 states
   c. change every year
   d. represent 48 states

2. The flag of the United States
   a. has 50 stripes
   b. has red stars
   c. has red and white stripes
   d. has never been changed

3. The flag of the United States
   a. has always had 50 stars
   b. was first made in the 1900s
   c. is red, white, and blue
   d. has four different colors

4. The "Pledge of Allegiance"
   a. was created by George Washington
   b. represents the 50 states
   c. is used to show respect for the flag
   d. was originally created in 1777

USING NEW WORDS

Use words from the reading passage to fill in the blanks. Follow the example on page 9.

Example: A symbol of a country: ___flag_____ (*paragraph 6*)

1. There are 13 of these on the American flag: _____

   (*paragraph 3*)

2. There are 50 of these on the American flag: _____

   (*paragraph 4*)

3. New; recent: _____ (*paragraph 5*)

4. To show that you care about something: to show _____

   (*paragraph 6*)

The original flag had 13 stars for the 13 colonies.

THINK ABOUT THE AMERICAN FLAG

1. Why are there 50 stars on the flag?

2. Why are there 13 stripes on the flag?

3. Why do you think that the flag is often seen on public buildings?

4. Why do you think that many Americans put flags in front of their houses on the Fourth of July?

5. Why do you think that the flag is considered to be important?

Answers for this chapter start on page 111.

EXPRESS YOUR IDEAS

Why do you think that many people have great respect for the flag?

Answers will vary.

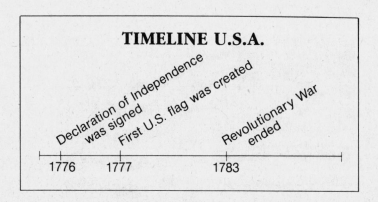

TIMELINE U.S.A.

Declaration of Independence was signed

First U.S. flag was created

Revolutionary War ended

1776   1777   1783

Chapter 9
The War of 1812 and the "Star-Spangled Banner"

Francis Scott Key saw the American flag flying over Fort McHenry.

BEFORE YOU READ

1. What is the name of the national anthem (song) of your native country?

2. Is there a story about the national anthem of your native country?

3. What is the name of the national anthem of the United States?

4. When can you hear the national anthem of the United States?

5. Think about relations between the United States and England after the Revolutionary War. Do you think that relations were good or bad? Why?

37

The War of 1812 and the National Anthem

In 1793, England and France went to war with each other. As the war progressed, England needed more soldiers. At the same time, many English citizens were working on American sailing ships.

England began to stop the American ships. The English would take their own citizens off the ships and send them to war. Sometimes the English also took Americans from the ships, and this angered the United States.

At that time, the United States also believed that the English were supporting Native Americans who were fighting against Americans. This was another reason that the United States was angry with England. Also, some Americans wanted a war with England: they thought that the U.S. could take over English territory in North America.

Tensions between the United States and England led to the War of 1812, which lasted from 1812 to 1814. There were no clear winners or losers in this war. The Americans and the English fought battles both in North America and on the Atlantic Ocean. At one point in the war, the English invaded the city of Washington and set fire to the White House.

On the night of September 13, 1814, the English navy bombarded Fort McHenry, in the state of Maryland. An American, Francis Scott Key, observed the battle.

It was raining during the battle, and Key could not see if the Americans were winning. In the morning, though, he saw that the American flag was flying. Fort McHenry had not lost the fight.

Francis Scott Key was inspired when he saw the flag, and he wrote a poem that became known as the "Star-Spangled Banner." The "Star-Spangled Banner" describes the American flag at the battle of Fort McHenry. It is now the national song, or anthem, of the United States.

AFTER YOU READ

Choose the best answer to complete the sentence.

1. England stopped American ships
   a. to collect taxes
   b. to take English citizens
   c. to take weapons
   d. to look for French sailors

2. The U.S. became angry when the English
   a. won the Revolutionary War
   b. fought with the French
   c. would not buy American products
   d. took Americans from American ships

3. The War of 1812 was fought

    a. in Europe
    b. by the French
    c. after the Revolutionary War
    d. for five years

4. The "Star-Spangled Banner" was written

    a. by an English sailor
    b. after a battle
    c. in the White House
    d. during the Revolutionary War

USING NEW WORDS

Use words from the reading passage to fill in the blanks. Follow the example on page 9.

Example: Land that belongs to a country: _territory_

(*paragraph 3*)

1. Continued or went on: _____ (*paragraph 1*)

2. Watched: _____ (*paragraph 5*)

3. A fight or struggle in a war: _____ (*paragraph 5*)

4. A symbol of a country: _____ (*paragraph 6*)

5. The national song of a country: _____ (*paragraph 7*)

Star-Spangled Banner

Oh say, can you see, by the dawn's early light,
What so proudly we hailed at the twilight's last gleaming?
Whose broad stripes and bright stars, through the perilous fight,
O'er the ramparts we watched, were so gallantly streaming!
And the rockets' red glare, the bombs bursting in air,
Gave proof through the night that our flag was still there.
Oh say, does that star-spangled banner yet wave
O'er the land of the free and the home of the brave?

THINK ABOUT THE WAR OF 1812

Answer the following questions.

1. Why was the United States angry with England?

2. Why did the English take their citizens from American ships?

3. What happened to the White House during the War of 1812?

4. What inspired Francis Scott Key to write the "Star-Spangled Banner"?

5. Which were the two wars that the United States fought against England?

Answers for this chapter start on page 111.

EXPRESS YOUR IDEAS

In the years since the War of 1812, the United States and England have developed good relations. Why do you think this has happened?

Answers will vary.

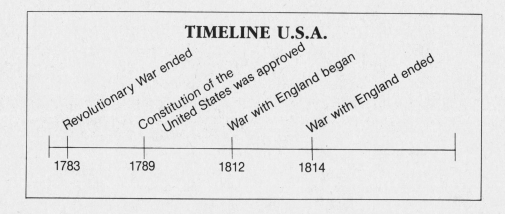

TIMELINE U.S.A.

Revolutionary War ended — 1783

Constitution of the United States was approved — 1789

War with England began — 1812

War with England ended — 1814

Chapter 10
Abraham Lincoln and the Civil War

Harriet Tubman, at the left, helped many slaves escape to freedom.

BEFORE YOU READ

1. What is a civil war? How is it different from *other* kinds of war?

2. Why is a civil war hard for a country?

3. Who fought in the American Civil War?

4. What is a slave? Where did slaves in the United States come from?

5. Who was Abraham Lincoln?

A Nation Divided and a President Lost

Abraham Lincoln was born on a farm in the state of Kentucky on February 12, 1809. Lincoln's family was very poor, and he worked hard at manual jobs to support his family. Lincoln loved books and would walk long distances to find books to read.

In 1861, Lincoln became the sixteenth president of the United States. At that time, there were big differences between the Northern and the Southern states. The main difference was that the economy of the South was based on farming. Much of this work was done by slaves who planted and picked crops like tobacco and cotton.

The slaves were the descendants of Africans who had been forced onto slave ships and brought to the New World. Slaves could be bought and sold like property. They were not free to travel or work wherever they wanted. Many times husbands, wives, and children were separated from each other.

Unlike that of the South, the economy of the North was not based on slavery. The North was beginning to produce manufactured goods in factories. The factories made clothing, furniture, machinery, and other things to be bought and sold. Many Northerners opposed the system of slavery and wanted to end it.

The Southern states decided to separate from the United States and form their own country where slavery would be permitted. The South was called the Confederacy and the North was called the Union. In April 1861, Confederate soldiers attacked Fort Sumter in South Carolina, and the Civil War began.

Abraham Lincoln was dedicated to keeping the United States together as one nation. In the middle of the Civil War, Lincoln signed the Emancipation Proclamation, a document that ended slavery in the Southern states. As a result, many slaves stopped working or even ran away to the North. This action weakened the South, and it helped the North win the war.

The Civil War lasted from 1861 to 1865, and more than half a million people died in the war. The years of the war were an emotional time in the United States, and many people hated Abraham Lincoln. In April 1865, while Lincoln was still president, he was killed by an assassin.

AFTER YOU READ

Choose the best answer to complete the sentence.

1. Abraham Lincoln was

   a. the sixteenth president
   b. a soldier in the Civil War
   c. born to a rich family
   d. killed in 1900

2. The Civil War

   a. brought slavery to the U.S.
   b. was won by the South
   c. was fought against England
   d. ended in 1865

3. The Emancipation
Proclamation

    a. started the Civil War
    b. gave freedom to some slaves
    c. lasted from 1861 to 1865
    d. made slavery legal

4. The Northern states

    a. had no factories
    b. fought against Canada
    c. wanted to keep slavery
    d. won the Civil War

USING NEW WORDS

Choose from the words below to complete the sentences.

        economy   introduced   opposed   property
        descendants   slavery   separated

1. The _____ of the South was based on farming.

2. Today, people can't be bought and sold in the United

    States. _____ is illegal.

3. Slaves were _____ of people from Africa because they

    were their children, grandchildren, and great-grandchildren.

4. Slaves were thought of as _____, just like land.

5. Many Northerners _____ slavery because it's wrong.

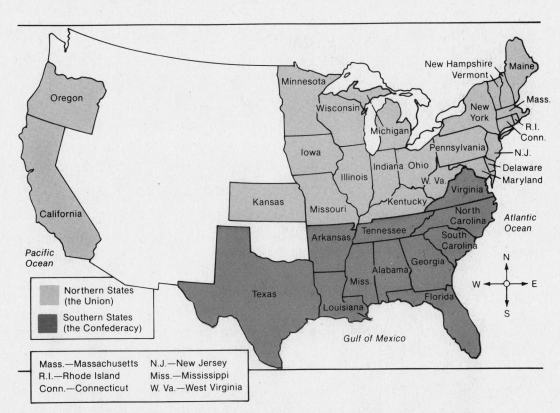

This map shows how the United States was divided during the Civil War.

43

THINK ABOUT THE CIVIL WAR

Answer the following questions.

1. What was an important difference between the Northern and Southern states?

2. What happened to Lincoln to end his presidency?

3. Why do you think that Lincoln is considered a great president?

4. Why did many people in the South support the use of slavery?

5. Think of the economy of the Northern states. Why do you think that the North was able to win the war?

Answers for this chapter start on page 112.

EXPRESS YOUR IDEAS

Do you think slavery would have ended if the South had won the Civil War? Explain.

Answers will vary.

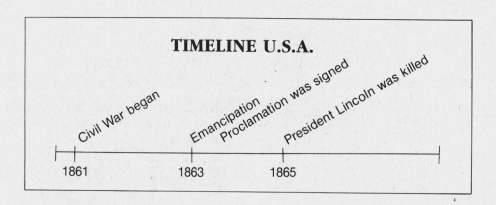

TIMELINE U.S.A.

Civil War began

Emancipation Proclamation was signed

President Lincoln was killed

1861   1863   1865

Chapter 11
Expansion and
Immigration

Many immigrants came to the United States to start a new life.

BEFORE YOU READ

1. Why do people come to live in the United States?

2. Where do you think most immigrants come from today?

3. Do you know where immigrants came from in the past?

4. Do you know why immigrants came here in the past?

5. Today there are 50 states in the United States. Were there always 50 states?

The Expansion of the United States

At the end of the 1700s, the territory of the United States extended west from the Atlantic Ocean to the Mississippi River. Then, in 1803, France sold a huge area of land to the United States. This land was called the Louisiana Purchase.

The Louisiana Purchase reached west from the Mississippi River to the Rocky Mountains and included the areas between Canada and the Gulf of Mexico. It made the United States almost two times as big as it had been before.

In 1848, after a war with Mexico, the United States took possession of land between the Rocky Mountains and the Pacific Ocean. The United States now extended from the Atlantic Ocean to the Pacific Ocean.

The federal government helped develop the American West. The government encouraged the construction of railroads and sold land in the West cheaply to get people to move there. Also, many people moved west to look for gold.

In 1845, Texas became part of the United States. Texas is the second largest state in the United States. The largest state is Alaska, which Russia sold to the United States in 1867. The last territories to become states were Alaska and Hawaii, in 1959.

The expansion of the United States was accompanied by heavy immigration. In the 1800s, millions of Europeans crossed the Atlantic Ocean to live in the United States. Most of these immigrants were poor and lived in crowded conditions. Even the children worked long hours in factories.

Today, fewer immigrants come from European countries. The majority of immigrants to the United States now come from other parts of the world, from countries such as Vietnam, the Philippines, and Mexico. Many immigrants come for economic or political reasons.

AFTER YOU READ

Choose the best answer to complete the sentence.

1. The Louisiana Purchase

   a. included the 13 colonies
   b. included Alaska
   c. was bought from France
   d. was made in 1848

2. The state of Alaska

   a. was part of the Louisiana Purchase
   b. is the second largest state in the U.S.
   c. became a state in 1859
   d. was purchased from Russia

3. The second largest state in the U.S. is

   a. Alaska
   b. Texas
   c. Hawaii
   d. Louisiana

4. In the 1800s, most immigrants came from

   a. Europe
   b. Vietnam
   c. the Philippines
   d. Mexico

USING NEW WORDS

Use words from the reading passage to fill in the blanks. Follow the example on page 9.

Example: An area of land belonging to a country: _territory_

(*paragraph 1*)

1. Reached from one place to another: _____ (*paragraph 3*)

2. To make bigger or better: _____ (*paragraph 4*)

3. People who go to live in another country: _____

   (*paragraph 6*)

4. A growth or increase in size: _____ (*paragraph 6*)

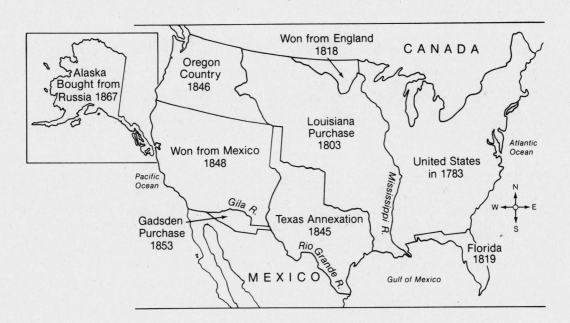

The expansion of the U.S. from 1783 to 1867.

THINK ABOUT THE EXPANSION OF THE UNITED STATES

Answer the following questions.

1. What area was included in the Louisiana Purchase?

2. What area was acquired after a war with Mexico?

3. Where do many immigrants to the United States come from today?

4. Why do immigrants come to the United States?

5. Why do you think that immigrants came to the United States in the 1800s?

Answers for this chapter start on page 112.

EXPRESS YOUR IDEAS

Why did you come to the U.S.? What are some reasons why people you know came to the U.S.?

Answers will vary.

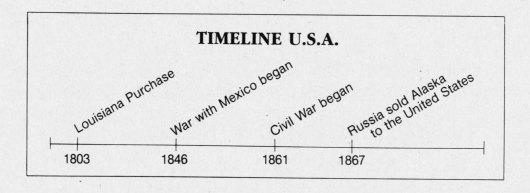

TIMELINE U.S.A.

Louisiana Purchase — 1803

War with Mexico began — 1846

Civil War began — 1861

Russia sold Alaska to the United States — 1867

Chapter 12
The United States in the World Wars

These soliders are saying good-bye to their loved ones as they go off to war.

BEFORE YOU READ

1. Why have two wars been called world wars?

2. When was World War I? When was World War II?

3. Do you know who fought in these wars? Did your native country fight in these wars?

4. Were either of these wars fought on U.S. land?

5. Think about the power of the United States in the world. Do you think the U.S. was stronger or weaker after the world wars?

The United States and the World Wars

In 1914, World War I began in Europe. A group of nations including England and France went to war against another group of nations including Germany and Austria-Hungary.

At first, most Americans wanted to remain neutral. They did not want to fight in a war on another continent. But it was hard to stay neutral. Although no American soldiers were fighting, the United States helped England and France, sending them food and other goods by ship.

In 1917, American ships were attacked by German warships, and the United States finally went to war. The United States helped England and France fight against Germany and Austria-Hungary.

When the war ended in 1918, the United States had great economic and political power. American industry was greatly developed by the war. The country could produce enormous amounts of manufactured goods such as automobiles and airplanes.

Like World War I, World War II began in Europe. Adolf Hitler, the leader of Germany, and Benito Mussolini, the leader of Italy, wanted to rule all of Europe. The United States tried to stay out of the war. But then Japan, which supported Germany and Italy, attacked the United States.

On December 7, 1941, the Japanese bombed an American naval base in Hawaii called Pearl Harbor. The United States declared war on Japan. Later, the United States also entered the war in Europe, where a group of nations including the United States, England, and the Soviet Union fought against Germany and Italy.

By May 1945, Germany and Italy had surrendered, but Japan was still fighting. During the war, the United States had invented the first atomic bomb. In August 1945, the United States dropped the bomb on two cities in Japan. The cities were destroyed, and hundreds of thousands of people died. After this, Japan surrendered to end the war.

After World War II, the United States became a dominant power in the world. As a result, American culture and influence began to be felt around the world.

AFTER YOU READ

Choose the best answer to complete the sentence.

1. In World War I, the United States

   a. did not participate
   b. lost to Germany
   c. used the atomic bomb
   d. was neutral at first

2. The United States entered World War I after

   a. it was attacked by Germany
   b. it was attacked by Japan
   c. Germany surrendered
   d. Italy surrendered

3. In World War II, the U.S.

   a. was attacked by Japan
   b. attacked a naval base in Hawaii
   c. fought against England
   d. fought against Austria-Hungary

4. After World War II, the United States

   a. developed the atomic bomb
   b. entered the war in Europe
   c. lost its economic power
   d. had a dominant position in the world

USING NEW WORDS

Choose from the words below to complete the sentences.

naval   atomic bomb   involved   influence   neutral
continent   invented

1. The United States didn't want to take sides in the war; it wanted to stay _____.

2. U.S. ships were bombed at the _____ base called Pearl Harbor.

3. The _____ can kill thousands of people at a time.

4. The United States created, or _____, the atomic bomb.

5. American products and music have had a great _____ on the rest of the world.

The United States entered World War II after the bombing of Pearl Harbor.

51

THINK ABOUT THE WORLD WARS

Answer the following questions.

1. When did the United States enter World War I?

2. Who did the United States fight against in World War II?

3. The United States used the atomic bomb against which country?

4. Why do you think that American industries became stronger during the world wars?

5. How were other countries affected by World War II?

Answers for this chapter start on page 113.

EXPRESS YOUR IDEAS

As a result of the world wars, the United States became a very powerful country. How did you see the influence of the U.S. in your native country?

Answers will vary.

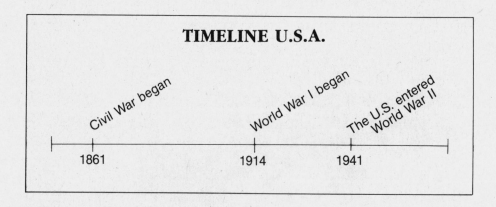

TIMELINE U.S.A.

Civil War began

World War I began

The U.S. entered World War II

1861   1914   1941

Chapter Review 2

WORD FIND

All of the words in the list are hidden in the box. They go from left to right and from top to bottom. Circle each one. One is done for you.

```
I   M   M   I   G   R   A   N   T
W   C   S   R   I   L   W   A   R
O   F   L   A   G   M   L   A   W
R   X   A   N   T   H   E   M   P
L   U   V   F   R   E   E   S   O
D   F   E   D   E   R   A   L   W
T   O   B   A   C   C   O   Y   E
S   U   R   R   E   N   D   E   R
```

✔ FEDERAL
LAW
POWER
FLAG
ANTHEM
SLAVE
TOBACCO
FREE
IMMIGRANT
WORLD
SURRENDER
WAR

TIMELINE

Put the events in the correct order on the timeline.

U.S. Constitution was written
World War I began
World War II ended
Civil War ended

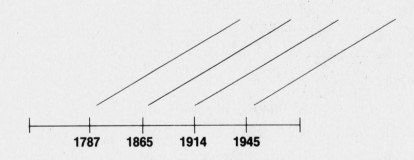

1787   1865   1914   1945

MAP ACTIVITY

On the map below, mark these places. Look back at page 47 if you need help.

1. Mexico
2. Canada
3. Mississippi River

4. Gulf of Mexico
5. Atlantic Ocean
6. Pacific Ocean

QUIZ

Find a partner and practice answering these questions.

1. What is the Constitution?

2. When was the Constitution adopted?

3. What is the "Star-Spangled Banner"?

4. Who wrote the "Star-Spangled Banner"?

5. What was the Civil War?

6. Who was the president during the Civil War?

7. Which side won the Civil War?

8. What happened to Lincoln after the Civil War ended?

9. Why did immigrants come to the United States in the late 1800s and the early 1900s?

10. Why did the United States enter World War II?

Answers for this chapter review start on page 113.

U.S. Government

These new U.S. citizens celebrate.

Chapter 13
What Is Democracy?

A man speaks out at a town meeting in his community.

BEFORE YOU READ

1. What is democracy?

2. What is an election?

3. Do you think that it is important to vote? Why?

4. In a democracy, what are "rights"?

5. What helps keep a democracy strong?

Democracy and Constitutional Rights

In the first part of this book, you read about the history of the United States. Now we will look at the government of the United States. Let's begin with some basic questions:

What is democracy?

Democracy is a type of government. In a democracy, citizens are the final authority in government. Citizens control the government.

How do citizens control their government in a democracy?

Democracy in the United States is called representative democracy. In a representative democracy, citizens choose representatives in elections. These men and women become members of the government.

Elections are held on a regular basis. In this way, citizens have regular opportunities to change the government.

What do representatives do?

Representatives make decisions for the citizens. They make these decisions based on the views and needs of the people. Representatives also decide on governmental issues and help protect the rights of citizens.

What are rights?

The Constitution of the United States contains a list of rights that all people possess. The government cannot take these rights away from people. Some of the most important rights include the rights to:

- speak freely
- believe in any religion
- own property
- not be cruelly punished by the government
- have a fair trial in a court

AFTER YOU READ

Choose the best answer to complete the sentence.

1. In a democracy,
   a. citizens control the government
   b. the government elects representatives
   c. the final authority is the government
   d. the government controls the citizens

2. In a democracy, representatives are chosen by
   a. the president
   b. the government
   c. the military
   d. the citizens

3. In a representative democracy,

    a. representatives choose citizens in elections

    b. there is no way to change the government

    c. citizens elect members of the government

    d. the government elects citizens

4. Under the Constitution, people cannot

    a. believe in any religion

    b. speak against the government

    c. be put in jail without a trial

    d. own property

USING NEW WORDS

Choose from the words below to complete the sentences.

democracy   practiced   issues   government   protect   elect   right

1. Citizens have the _____ to believe in any religion.

2. Representatives should _____ people's rights.

3. _____ is a type of government.

4. In a democracy, the _____ is controlled by the people.

5. Citizens _____ representatives in the United States.

Democracy allows people to speak out for their rights.

59

THINK ABOUT DEMOCRACY

Answer the following questions.

1. What is democracy?

2. How do representatives become members of the government?

3. What are three important rights described in the Constitution?

4. Why are elections important?

5. Why do you think it is important for citizens to vote?

Answers for this chapter start on page 114.

EXPRESS YOUR IDEAS

Think of one important decision made by representatives in the government. Was this decision good or bad? Why?

Answers will vary.

IN THE U.S.A. . . .

More than 89 million Americans voted in the election for president in 1988.

Chapter 14
The U.S. Constitution

Congress makes laws.

Judges explain laws.

BEFORE YOU READ

1. What do you think should be the most important rules in a government?

2. What is the United States Constitution?

3. In which year was the Constitution created?

4. Why do you think the Constitution is called the "highest law of the land"?

5. Is the original Constitution still used today?

The United States Constitution

The original Constitution of the United States was adopted in 1789. The Constitution is a description of how the American government functions. Although the Constitution is 200 years old, it is still used today.

An important aspect of the original Constitution is its division of power. The Constitution divided power by creating three distinct areas, or branches, of government: the executive, the legislative, and the judicial.

The executive branch includes the president and vice president. The legislative branch includes the U.S. Congress. The judicial branch includes the system of courts and judges.

The Constitution gives different responsibilities to each of the branches. One branch of government cannot take the responsibilities of another branch. This division of responsibility gives stability to the American government; no area of government has too much power.

Since the original Constitution was adopted, there have been changes added to it. These changes are referred to as amendments. In 1791, 10 amendments were added to the Constitution. These 10 amendments are known as the Bill of Rights. The Bill of Rights is a list of rights that are guaranteed to the people of the United States.

In the years since the Bill of Rights was created, 16 other amendments have been added to the Constitution. There are now 26 amendments. The latest amendment was added in 1971.

AFTER YOU READ

Choose the best answer to complete the sentence.

1. The United States Constitution

   a. is 100 years old
   b. created four branches of government
   c. is a branch of government
   d. is still used today

2. The three branches of government

   a. all have too much power
   b. were created by the Constitution
   c. have the same responsibilities
   d. choose the president in elections

3. The legislative branch of government

   a. created the Constitution
   b. includes the Congress
   c. was created by the president
   d. has more power than the other branches

4. The Bill of Rights

   a. was added to the Constitution
   b. includes 26 amendments
   c. does not affect the government
   d. was adopted in 1789

USING NEW WORDS

Choose from the words below to complete the sentences.

branches   judges   responsibilities   discuss   stability
original   amendments   guarantees

1. In 1789, the _____ Constitution was adopted.

2. The Constitution created three _____ of government.

3. Each area of the government has its own _____.

4. Courts and _____ are part of the judicial branch.

5. The Bill of Rights _____ certain rights to the people.

6. The Bill of Rights consists of 10 _____ to the

Constitution.

Federal Government	State Governments
• makes national laws • rules on important court cases • directs relations with other countries • distributes money to the states	• support local schools • build highways and prisons • look after public health • provide welfare for the poor

These are some of the duties of the federal government and of state governments.

THINK ABOUT THE U.S. CONSTITUTION

Answer the following questions.

1. What is the Constitution?

2. Why did the Constitution create three branches of government?

3. What are the three branches of government?

4. How does the Constitution help make the American government stable?

5. Why do you think that the Constitution has been changed, or amended?

Answers for this chapter start on page 114.

EXPRESS YOUR IDEAS

The Constitution is only a document consisting of several pieces of paper, yet for 200 years it has been accepted as the supreme law of the United States. Why do you think that people continue to accept the Constitution? What would happen if the government or the people began to ignore the Constitution?

Answers will vary.

IN THE U.S.A. . . .
The United States Constitution is the oldest constitution that is still used.

Chapter 15
Three Branches of
U.S. Government

Former President John F. Kennedy speaking to Congress and the Supreme Court.

BEFORE YOU READ

1. In your native country, who is the most powerful person in the government?

2. How can a person become the leader of a government?

3. What are the three branches of government in the United States?

4. Do you think one branch is more important than the others?

5. Why do you think there are three branches?

The Three Branches of Government

In the last chapter, we discussed the three branches of the United States government. Each of these branches has different responsibilities.

The executive branch, which includes the president and vice president, works to put laws into effect. The president must make sure that laws are respected and obeyed.

The legislative branch, which includes the Congress, creates laws. The Congress consists of the House of Representatives and the Senate. New laws are created when both the House of Representatives and the Senate vote to approve them.

The judicial branch, which includes the court system and the Supreme Court, interprets laws. The judicial branch decides whether a law is allowed by the Constitution. The judicial branch also punishes lawbreakers.

Here is an example of how the three branches of government interact:

Imagine that Congress creates a law that affects workers. The Department of Labor, which is under the president's control, would make sure that the law is obeyed.

If someone believes that the law is not allowed by the Constitution, the judicial branch becomes involved. The Supreme Court—part of the judicial branch—can be asked to decide if the law is unconstitutional. An unconstitutional law is a law that is prohibited by the Constitution.

This example shows how all three branches of government can interact, with each branch exercising a different responsibility.

AFTER YOU READ

Choose the best answer to complete the sentence.

1. The executive branch of government
   a. includes the Congress
   b. interprets laws
   c. does not have responsibilities
   d. makes sure that laws are obeyed

2. The legislative branch
   a. includes the vice president
   b. cannot create laws
   c. includes the Congress
   d. can decide if a law is unconstitutional

3. The judicial branch

    a. can decide that a law is unconstitutional

    b. has the same responsibilities as Congress

    c. controls the Department of Labor

    d. is divided into three branches

4. All three branches of government

    a. punish lawbreakers

    b. have the same responsibilities

    c. create laws

    d. interact with each other

USING NEW WORDS

Use words from the reading passage to fill in the blanks.

Example: The vice president is part of this branch of government:

<u>executive</u>   <u>branch</u>   *(paragraph 2)*

The **executive branch**, which includes the president and vice president, works to put laws into effect.

1. This branch of government includes the

    Congress: _____ *(paragraph 3)*

2. This branch of government includes the court system:

    _____ *(paragraph 4)*

3. Not allowed by the Constitution: _____ *(paragraph 7)*

4. To work together: _____ *(paragraph 8)*

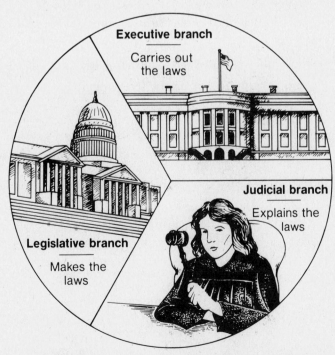

The three branches of government work together.

THINK ABOUT THE THREE BRANCHES
OF GOVERNMENT

Answer the following questions.

1. Why is power divided among the different branches of government?

2. What does the legislative branch of government do?

3. Which branch of government punishes people who break the law?

4. Which branch of government decides if a law is permitted by the Constitution?

5. Which branch of government would control the Department of Transportation?

Answers for this chapter start on page 114.

EXPRESS YOUR IDEAS

Think of the different responsibilities of the three branches of government. If you could work in any branch of government, which would you choose? Why?

Answers will vary.

IN THE U.S.A. . . .

The three branches of government have some control over each other. For instance, the president and the Senate have the power to choose the judges of the Supreme Court. But the Supreme Court has the power to say that laws made by the Senate and the president are unconstitutional.

Chapter 16
The Executive Branch

The president of the United States lives and works in the White House.

BEFORE YOU READ

1. Who is the president or leader of your native country?

2. Who were some of the most famous U.S. presidents? Who is the president now?

3. What does the president do?

4. If something happened to the president, who would take his place?

5. What do you think are characteristics of a good president?

The Executive Branch

The executive branch of American government is headed by the president. The executive branch also includes the vice president and the president's cabinet. The president lives and works in the White House in Washington, D.C.

The president and vice president are elected every four years in national elections. A person cannot be elected president more than twice.

The president has many responsibilities that make him the single most important person in the American government. The president has to verify that the laws of the nation are obeyed. He is also the commander in chief of the military. Another important duty of the president is maintaining diplomatic relations with other nations.

The vice president is perhaps the second most important person in the U.S. government. The vice president takes the place of the president if the president dies, becomes too sick to work, or quits. For example, in 1963, Lyndon Johnson became president after the assassination of President Kennedy.

The vice president is also the head of the Senate. If the Senate reaches a tie during a vote, the vice president can vote in order to break the tie.

The executive branch of government also includes 14 departments, such as the Department of Agriculture, the Department of Transportation, and the Department of Defense. These departments help the president control important areas of government.

The heads of the 14 departments regularly meet with the president. These department heads form what is referred to as the president's cabinet. The heads of most of the departments are called secretaries. For example, there is a Secretary of Agriculture and a Secretary of Transportation.

AFTER YOU READ

Choose the best answer to complete the sentence.

1. The president of the United States
   a. is part of the legislative branch
   b. is elected every eight years
   c. is the head of the Senate
   d. is the head of the military

2. The president is *not* responsible for
   a. making sure laws are obeyed
   b. the military
   c. diplomatic relations
   d. writing new laws

3. The vice president
   a. lives in the White House
   b. is commander in chief of the military
   c. can vote in the Senate
   d. is elected by the Senate

4. The president's cabinet
   a. meets with the president
   b. can vote in the Senate
   c. can assume the role of the president
   d. includes 15 departments

USING NEW WORDS

Use words from the reading passage to fill in the blanks. Follow the example on page 67.

Example: This group meets regularly with the president:

___cabinet___ (*paragraph 7*)

1. The president lives in this building:

_____ _____ (*paragraph 1*)

2. To make sure about something: _____ (*paragraph 3*)

3. The army, navy, and air force are members of this group:

_____ (*paragraph 3*)

4. A responsibility or an obligation: _____ (*paragraph 3*)

5. This occurs when the number of "yes" and "no" votes is the same:

_____ (*paragraph 5*)

The 41st president of the United States is George Bush.

THINK ABOUT THE EXECUTIVE BRANCH

Answer the following questions.

1. What are three important divisions of the executive branch?
2. What are some responsibilities of the president?
3. What are some responsibilities of the vice president?
4. Why do you think that the president regularly meets with cabinet members?
5. Why do you think that there is a limit on the number of years that a person can be president?

Answers for this chapter start on page 115.

EXPRESS YOUR IDEAS

Think of the responsibilities of a president. Describe what you think are the most important qualities of a good president. Also, describe qualities that you think are not desirable in a president.

Answers will vary.

IN THE U.S.A. . . .

The first cabinet was created by George Washington. There were three cabinet members at that time.

Chapter 17
The Legislative Branch

Former Mexican President José Lopez Portillo addresses the U.S. Congress.

BEFORE YOU READ

1. Do you know the names of the senators in your state?

2. What is the legislative branch of the national government?

3. What does the legislative branch do?

4. How do people become members of the legislative branch?

5. Where does the legislative branch work?

The Legislative Branch

When the Constitution was first written in 1787, there was a need to solve a problem. States with low populations wanted a Congress in which each state would have the same number of representatives. These states were afraid that the larger states would have too much power in the government.

But states with large populations wanted each state to be represented on the basis of the population of that state. In that way, larger states would have more representatives in Congress.

This problem was solved by the creation of two houses of Congress. In the House of Representatives, the number of representatives for the state is based on its population. In the Senate, each state has only two senators, no matter how large or small it is.

For instance, Texas, which has a large population, had 27 representatives in 1988. Alaska, which has a small population, had only one representative. In the Senate, however, each state has exactly two senators.

Members of the House of Representatives are elected for terms of two years. Currently, there are 435 members of the House of Representatives. Members of the Senate are elected for terms of six years. In all, there are 100 senators.

A law begins when either house of Congress creates a bill. A bill is an idea for a new law. If both houses of Congress agree on a bill, they send the bill to the president.

If the president agrees that a bill is a good idea, he signs the bill, and it becomes a law. If the president disagrees with a bill, he can veto it, or turn it down. If a bill is vetoed by the president, it can become a law only if two-thirds of each house of Congress approves the bill a second time.

AFTER YOU READ

Choose the best answer to complete the sentence.

1. In the House of Representatives, states with large populations

   a. have more representatives
   b. have 100 senators
   c. have the same number of representatives
   d. hold elections every six years

2. In the Senate

   a. there are 435 members
   b. members can veto a bill
   c. there were 27 senators in 1988
   d. there are 100 members

3. The president
  a. sends bills to Congress
  b. chooses the two senators from each state
  c. can veto bills created by Congress
  d. votes in the Congress

4. The two houses of Congress
  a. have the same number of members
  b. have only one member from Alaska
  c. send bills to the president
  d. are part of the executive branch

USING NEW WORDS

Choose from the words below to complete the sentences.

solved   agree   veto   bills   term   written   population

1. A problem was _____ by the creation of two houses of Congress.

2. Congress sends _____ to the president for approval.

3. The _____ of a senator is six years.

4. The president can _____ a bill.

5. Since many people live in California, the state is known for its large

_____ .

	Senators	Representatives
How many are there?	100	435
How many from each state?	2 senators	It depends on how many people live in the state.
How long are their terms?	6 years	2 years
How old must they be?	30 years old	25 years old

This chart shows the differences between senators and representatives.

THINK ABOUT THE LEGISLATIVE BRANCH

Answer the following questions.

1. How many houses of Congress are there? What are the names of the houses of Congress?
2. How and why are the houses of Congress different?
3. Why does California have more members in the House of Representatives than Nevada?
4. How long is the term of a senator?
5. How long is the term of a representative?

Answers for this chapter start on page 115.

EXPRESS YOUR IDEAS

Do you think it is good that the president is involved in the creation of laws? Why?

Answers will vary.

IN THE U.S.A. . . .

When the Constitution was being written, there was a plan to create only one house of Congress. The smaller states wanted a Congress that would give all states the same number of representatives. The larger states wanted a Congress that would give larger states more representatives. The creation of the two houses is known as the "Great Compromise."

Chapter 18
The Judicial Branch

The Supreme Court of the United States is made up of nine judges called justices.

BEFORE YOU READ

1. Have you ever been in a court? What was it like?

2. What do judges do?

3. Why do you think that courts are necessary?

4. What do you think are important characteristics of a good judge?

5. Which is the most important court in the United States?

The Judicial Branch

The judicial branch of government consists of a system of courts and judges. These courts have two jobs: to interpret, or explain, the laws and to enforce the laws.

There are many different kinds of courts. For example, there are criminal courts and traffic courts. But the most important court in the United States is the Supreme Court. The Supreme Court judges, known as justices, examine laws. They decide if the Constitution permits the laws. If a law is not permitted by the Constitution, the law is unconstitutional.

There are nine judges on the Supreme Court. These justices can decide that lower courts have made an incorrect decision in a case. Then the justices can change, or override, the decision of the lower court. Final decisions on legal issues are made by a majority vote among the justices. To have a majority, at least five of the nine justices must agree.

The Supreme Court is located in Washington, D.C. The members of the Supreme Court can keep their jobs for life. Because the justices are in office for many years, the Supreme Court does not suddenly change its philosophy, or way of thinking. This gives stability to the Court.

New Supreme Court justices are chosen by the president. The president's choice, however, must be approved by the Senate.

AFTER YOU READ

Choose the best answer to complete the sentence.

1. The judicial branch of government
   a. includes the president
   b. submits bills to the president
   c. creates laws
   d. interprets laws

2. The Supreme Court
   a. does not interpret laws
   b. is the most important court in the United States
   c. is composed of members of Congress
   d. cannot override decisions of other courts

3. The Supreme Court
   a. includes 10 justices
   b. works in the White House
   c. can declare that a law is unconstitutional
   d. wrote the Constitution

4. The Supreme Court justices
   a. can keep their jobs for life
   b. can veto laws made by Congress
   c. have little effect on the other branches of government
   d. are elected every four years

USING NEW WORDS

Use words from the reading passage to fill in the blanks. Follow the example on page 67.

Example: This word describes a law that is not allowed by the Constitution: <u>unconstitutional</u> (*paragraph 2*)

1. These are interpreted in the

   courts: _____ (*paragraph 1*)

2. The person in charge of a court: _____

   (*paragraph 2*)

3. The title for the Supreme Court judges: _____ (*paragraph 2*)

4. More than half: _____ (*paragraph 3*)

5. Way of thinking: _____ (*paragraph 4*)

Two children sit in front of the Supreme Court building. The Supreme Court has made many decisions to guarantee equal education for Americans of all races.

THINK ABOUT THE JUDICIAL BRANCH

Answer the following questions.

1. How does a person become a member of the Supreme Court?

2. How does the Supreme Court make decisions?

3. Why is the Supreme Court the most important court in the United States?

4. Why do you think that Supreme Court judges can keep their jobs for life?

5. Why do you think that the Supreme Court is located in Washington, D.C.?

Answers for this chapter start on page 116.

EXPRESS YOUR IDEAS

Think about the responsibilities of a judge. What do you think are the characteristics of a good judge?

Answers will vary.

IN THE U.S.A. . . .

Since the time of George Washington, the president's choice for a new Supreme Court judge has been rejected by the Senate 27 times. In 1987, the Senate rejected Judge Robert Bork, who was chosen by President Reagan.

Chapter Review 3

WORD FIND

All of the words in the list are hidden in the box. They go from left to right and from top to bottom. Circle each one. One is done for you.

```
D  B  A  L  A  N  C  E  B
E  J  U  D  G  E  F  Z  R
M  P  R  O  T  E  C  T  A
O  L  B  I  L  L  I  C  N
C  A  B  I  N  E  T  O  C
R  W  V  Y  P  C  I  U  H
A  S  Q  T  U  T  Z  R  V
C  C  H  O  O  S  E  T  T
Y  R  I  G  H  T  N  U  R
```

✔ BALANCE
CABINET
BILL
LAWS
JUDGE
COURT
DEMOCRACY
CITIZEN
ELECT
PROTECT
RIGHT
CHOOSE
BRANCH

FIND OUT

Find out the names of these officials and write them down. Practice saying each name.

1. The president of the U.S.: _____

2. The vice president: _____

3. The senators from your state: _____

   and _____

4. The governor of your state: _____

5. Your congressman (the person who represents you in the House of

   Representatives): _____

MATCH-UP

Listed below are things that each branch of government does. Put each phrase in the correct box.

EXECUTIVE

1. _____
2. _____
3. _____

LEGISLATIVE

1. _____
2. _____
3. _____

JUDICIAL

1. _____
2. _____
3. _____

writes new laws

punishes people who break
the law

runs the military

makes sure laws are obeyed

has senators and representatives

explains the laws

includes the cabinet

makes sure that laws agree with the
Constitution

has two parts, or houses

QUIZ

Find a partner and practice answering these questions.

1. What is the form of government in the U.S.?

2. How many branches are there in the U.S. government?

3. What does each branch do?

4. What are the two parts of Congress?

5. How many members are in the House of Representatives?

6. What is the term of office for a person in the House of Representatives?

7. How many members are there in the Senate?

8. What is the term of office for a U.S. senator?

9. What is the term of office for the president of the U.S.?

10. Who takes the president's place if he cannot finish his term?

11. How many times can a person be elected president?

12. What is the name of the highest court in the land?

13. Who picks the judges on this court?

14. How long can the judges serve?

15. Where is this court located?

Answers for this chapter review start on page 116.

Chapter 19
The Bill of Rights

The Bill of Rights guarantees Americans the right to a fair trial.

BEFORE YOU READ

1. The Bill of Rights is part of the Constitution. What are rights?

2. What rights are in the Constitution?

3. What rights are gained when a person becomes a permanent resident? a citizen?

4. Do you think it's important for a government to write down people's rights? Why?

5. The picture shows a jury trial. What could happen if a person is arrested and doesn't have the right to a trial?

Extending Protection—The Bill of Rights

In Chapter 14 you read about the addition of the Bill of Rights to the Constitution. The Bill of Rights consists of 10 amendments that were added to the Constitution in 1791.

The Bill of Rights describes basic rights of the people of the United States. The Bill of Rights was created because it is important to have a clear, written explanation of these rights.

The Constitution is the ultimate legal authority in the United States. The Bill of Rights is part of the Constitution; this means that the government must obey the Bill of Rights.

Among the important rights contained in the Bill of Rights are:

- the right to freedom of speech
- the right to freedom of religion
- the right to have a trial in court if you are accused of a crime
- the right to have a lawyer defend you in court
- the right to receive a fair, quick trial in court

While the Bill of Rights gives the people important freedoms, it also puts certain restrictions on the government. For instance, the Bill of Rights states that:

- the government cannot enter a person's home without special permission
- the government cannot cruelly punish a person who has broken the law

There are other rights and liberties protected by the Bill of Rights. In all, the Bill of Rights provides two kinds of protection for the people of the United States: it guarantees the rights of people, and it restricts the power of government over the people.

AFTER YOU READ

Choose the best answer to complete the sentence.

1. The Bill of Rights is
   a. older than the Constitution
   b. no longer used
   c. now part of the Constitution
   d. part of the Declaration of Independence

2. The Bill of Rights
   a. created three branches of government
   b. protects the rights of government
   c. protects the rights of the people
   d. allows the government to do anything

3. According to the Bill of Rights, if a person is accused of a crime, he

   a. loses his rights
   b. has a right to a fair trial
   c. has no rights
   d. must know the Bill of Rights

4. The Bill of Rights protects people's rights because

   a. it is part of the Constitution
   b. it was written many years ago
   c. it only contains 10 amendments
   d. it is difficult to understand

USING NEW WORDS

Choose from the words below to complete the sentences.

     court   basic   amendments   liberties   restrictions
           cruel   changed   trial   lawyer

1. A person has the right to a fair _____ in court.

2. The Constitution can be _____ by the use of

amendments.

3. The Bill of Rights says that the government cannot

be _____ to a person.

4. The Bill of Rights places _____ on the government.

5. A person accused of a crime has a right to be defended by

a _____.

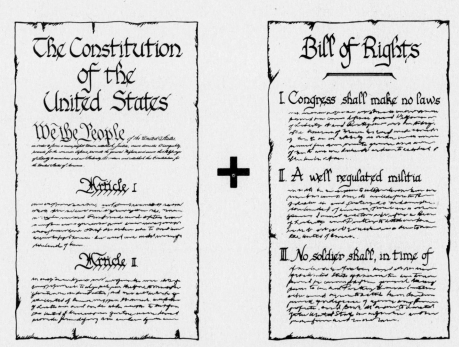

Together, the Constitution and the Bill of Rights are the basis of
American government and freedoms.

THINK ABOUT THE BILL OF RIGHTS

Answer the following questions.

1. When was the Bill of Rights added to the Constitution?

2. What is the Bill of Rights?

3. What are two kinds of protection that the Bill of Rights provides?

4. Why is the right to freedom of religion important?

5. Why is it good that the government cannot go into a person's house without special permission?

Answers for this chapter start on page 117.

EXPRESS YOUR IDEAS

Look back at the Bill of Rights. Which right is most important to you, and why?

Answers will vary.

IN THE U.S.A. . . .

The United States Bill of Rights is one of the world's three famous bills of rights:

- English Bill of Rights, 1689
- French Declaration of the Rights of Man and of the Citizen, 1789
- United States Bill of Rights, 1791

Chapter 20
Other Amendments to the Constitution

These women marched to gain the right to vote.

BEFORE YOU READ

1. How can the Constitution be changed?

2. What is the name of the first 10 amendments to the Constitution?

3. What are some of the rights in the Bill of Rights?

4. Why is it necessary to make changes in the Constitution?

5. In the past, some groups of people were not permitted to vote in the United States. Who were some of those groups?

Amending the Constitution

Since the Bill of Rights was created in 1791, other amendments have been added to the Constitution. There are now 26 amendments.

An amendment is difficult to create. An amendment can be created when two-thirds of each house of Congress approves the amendment. Then, the amendment must be approved by three-fourths of the 50 states.

Several amendments help to expand the rights of people in the United States. Some of these amendments include:

- Amendment 13 (1865)—Slavery is declared illegal.
- Amendment 15 (1870)—People of any race can vote.
- Amendment 19 (1920)—Women are allowed to vote.
- Amendment 24 (1964)—No person can be forced to pay money to vote for members of Congress or the president.
- Amendment 26 (1971)—Citizens 18 years old or older can vote.

Other amendments have been created to help the government function better. Some of these amendments include:

- Amendment 16 (1913)—Congress can tax the money people earn.
- Amendment 22 (1951)—A person cannot be elected president more than twice.

An amendment can be changed by another amendment. For example, in 1919, the Eighteenth Amendment prohibited the sale of alcohol. Then, in 1933, the Twenty-first Amendment legalized the sale of alcohol.

The prohibition and legalization of alcohol show that the Constitution is flexible. Amendments allow the Constitution to be adapted to social changes in the United States.

AFTER YOU READ

Choose the best answer to complete the sentence.

1. An amendment
   a. can be created easily
   b. can be created only if the president approves it
   c. is an addition to the Constitution
   d. can never be changed

2. Because of amendments, the Constitution
   a. is not necessary
   b. can reflect changes in American society
   c. does not need to be changed anymore
   d. is the same as it was in 1791

3. One result of the amendments is that

    a. people have to pay money to vote

    b. a president can stay in office for 12 years

    c. more people can vote

    d. Congress cannot make people pay taxes

4. An amendment must be approved by

    a. the vice president

    b. Congress

    c. the citizens

    d. the Supreme Court

USING NEW WORDS

Choose from the words below to complete the sentences.

earned   allowed   illegal   tax   function   flexible   expanded

1. People of any race are _____ to vote.

2. The Constitution is _____ and can be changed.

3. It is _____ to have slaves in the United States.

4. To get money, the government can _____ the citizens.

5. Some amendments help the government _____ better.

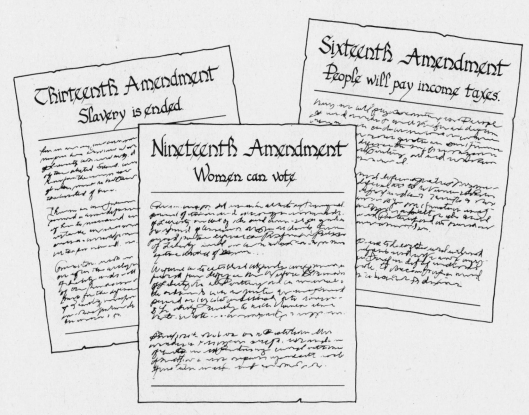

Altogether, there are 26 amendments to the U.S. Constitution.

THINK ABOUT THE AMENDMENTS TO THE CONSTITUTION

Answer the following questions.

1. How many amendments are there?

2. What are some amendments that make it easier for people to vote?

3. Which amendment provided the government with more money?

4. Why is it difficult to add new amendments to the Constitution?

5. Why do you think the Twenty-fourth Amendment was created?

Answers for this chapter start on page 117.

EXPRESS YOUR IDEAS

Which of the amendments do you think is most important? Why?

Answers will vary.

IN THE U.S.A. . . .

In 1972, Congress approved an amendment that stated that a person's rights should not be affected by his or her sex. However, this "Equal Rights Amendment" was not approved by three-fourths of the states, so it was not added to the Constitution.

Chapter 21
The Voting Process

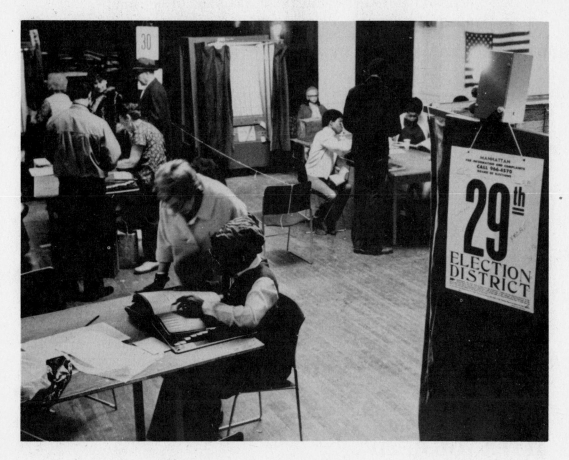

U.S. citizens can vote in local, state, and national elections.

BEFORE YOU READ

1. In your native country, do you have elections? What are they like?
2. What happens in an election in the United States?
3. How old must a person be to vote in the United States?
4. Do you think that every citizen should be allowed to vote? Why or why not?
5. Do you want to vote in elections in the United States?

Voting and Elections

The original Constitution permitted only certain people to vote. Since the Constitution was adopted, several amendments have been added to allow more citizens to vote. These amendments have given the right to vote to blacks, women, and all citizens who are 18 years old or older.

Citizens can vote in many elections. There are national elections for the president and vice president. In state elections, governors, senators, and other representatives of a state are chosen. Finally, there are local elections for leaders such as mayors and members of councils.

In an election, there are usually two or more candidates. A candidate is a person who wants to be elected to a position in government. A candidate is usually a member of a political party.

There are many different political parties in the United States, but the dominant parties are the Democratic Party and the Republican Party. Political parties have different philosophies about government and how government should work. The parties work to have their candidates elected; this allows the parties to extend their influence in the government.

To be able to vote in elections, a person must be a registered voter and a citizen of the United States. A citizen can register to vote at the offices of his or her community government. Registering to vote is a simple process and requires only a few minutes' time.

To help ensure that elections are honest, it is illegal to force any person to vote for a certain candidate. Also, a person's vote is a secret: neither the government nor any other person is allowed to discover how a citizen voted.

AFTER YOU READ

Choose the best answer to complete the sentence.

1. In the United States,
   a. all people can vote
   b. women have always been allowed to vote
   c. citizens under 18 years of age can vote
   d. more people can vote today because of amendments to the Constitution

2. In state elections,
   a. there is only one party
   b. the president is chosen
   c. there is only one candidate
   d. a governor can be elected

3. A person who wants to vote

    a. must be registered to vote
    b. can register at any location
    c. can vote in national elections only
    d. can vote in local elections only

4. A person's vote is known by

    a. the federal government
    b. the local government
    c. the political parties
    d. the voter only

USING NEW WORDS

Choose from the words below to complete the sentences.

voter   philosophies   candidates   registered
secret   parties   several

1. People vote for _____ in an election.

2. There are two major political _____ in the United

States.

3. Citizens must be _____ before they can vote.

4. A _____ must be at least 18 years old.

5. A person's vote is a _____.

Before citizens can vote, they must register.

THINK ABOUT VOTING AND ELECTIONS

Answer the following questions.

1. What are the two largest political parties in the United States?

2. Who can vote in the United States?

3. Why were amendments about voting added to the Constitution?

4. Why do you think a person has to be registered to vote?

5. In the United States, citizens may vote if they want to, but they are not required to vote. Do you think that citizens *should* be required to vote?

Answers for this chapter start on page 118.

EXPRESS YOUR IDEAS

Suppose you do not like any of the candidates in an election. Which is better: not to vote at all, or to vote for the candidate that you think would do the best job? Explain your opinion.

Answers will vary.

IN THE U.S.A. . . .

Candidates in elections are usually members of the two main political parties. These political parties choose their candidates in special elections called primaries.

Chapter Review 4

WORD FIND

All of the words in the list below are hidden in the box. They go from left to right and from top to bottom. Circle each one. One is done for you.

```
K  A  F  C  R  U  E  L  S
M  M  L  F  T  L  Y  A  R
L  E  A  A  D  D  P  W  I
I  N  G  V  O  T  E  Y  G
B  D  C  O  U  R  T  E  H
E  M  P  A  R  T  Y  R  T
R  E  G  I  S  T  E  R  S
T  N  A  T  I  O  N  A  L
Y  T  R  I  A  L  P  O  R
```

✔AMENDMENT
LIBERTY
TRIAL
COURT
CRUEL
REGISTER
VOTE
NATIONAL
PARTY
FLAG
LAWYER
RIGHTS
ADD

MATCH-UP

Match each holiday to the correct date. If you need help, look at the calendar on page 106.

_____ 1. Memorial Day
_____ 2. Independence Day
_____ 3. Thanksgiving
_____ 4. Christmas
_____ 5. Labor Day
_____ 6. Columbus Day
_____ 7. Lincoln's Birthday
_____ 8. New Year's Day

a. January 1
b. February 12
c. last Monday in May
d. July 4
e. first Monday in September
f. second Monday in October
g. fourth Thursday in November
h. December 25

QUIZ

Find a partner and practice answering these questions.

1. Can the Constitution be changed?

2. How many amendments does the Constitution have?

3. What is the Bill of Rights?

4. What are two rights guaranteed by the Bill of Rights?

5. What are some other important amendments?

6. What are the requirements for voting?

7. What are the two major political parties?

Answers for this chapter review start on page 118.

Appendix 1

Commonly Asked Questions About U.S. History

1. What were the people who settled Plymouth called?
2. What holiday began with the Pilgrims?
3. Where were the first English settlements?
4. What was the Boston Tea Party?
5. Who was the first commander in chief of the American army?
6. How many original colonies became the United States?
7. How many original colonies can you name?
8. What is the Declaration of Independence?
9. What are the basic rights set forth in the Declaration of Independence?
10. Who wrote the Declaration of Independence?
11. On what date did the members of the Continental Congress meet to vote on the Declaration of Independence?
12. Who was the first president of the United States?
13. When is his birthday?
14. Who is called "The Father of His Country"?
15. What is the birthdate of the United States?
16. Why do we celebrate the Fourth of July?
17. Who was president when the Civil War was fought?
18. Name five states that belonged to the Union (the North).
19. Name five states that belonged to the Confederacy (the South).
20. What happened to Lincoln after the Civil War ended?
21. Which side won the Civil War?
22. What is the "Star-Spangled Banner"?
23. Who wrote the "Star-Spangled Banner"?
24. How did the writer of the "Star-Spangled Banner" feel about his country?
25. Name the first, third, and sixteenth presidents of the United States.

Answers to Questions About U.S. History

1. The people who settled Plymouth were called **Pilgrims**.

2. **Thanksgiving** began with the Pilgrims.

3. The first English settlements were in **Jamestown, Virginia**, and in **Plymouth, Massachusetts**.

4. In Boston, Massachusetts, **colonists dressed as Indians went on English ships and threw the cargo of tea into the water**. They did this to show they were unhappy with the tax.

5. The first commander of the American army was **George Washington**.

6. **Thirteen** original colonies became the United States.

7. The first 13 colonies were: **Connecticut, Delaware, Georgia, Maryland, Massachusetts, New Hampshire, New Jersey, New York, North Carolina, Pennsylvania, Rhode Island, South Carolina, and Virginia**.

8. The Declaration of Independence is **a document that declared our independence from England**.

9. The Declaration of Independence says that all people have the right to **life, liberty, and the pursuit of happiness**.

10. **Thomas Jefferson** wrote the Declaration of Independence.

11. **July 4, 1776**, was the date the members of the Continental Congress met to vote on the Declaration of Independence.

12. **George Washington** was the first president of the United States.

13. His birthday is **February 22**.

14. The "Father of His Country" is **George Washington**.

15. The birthdate of the United States is the **Fourth of July**, or **Independence Day**.

16. We celebrate the Fourth of July **to remember our independence from England**.

17. The president of the United States during the Civil War was **Abraham Lincoln**.

18. The states that belonged to the Union, or the North, were: **California, Connecticut, Delaware, Illinois, Indiana, Iowa, Kansas, Kentucky, Maine, Massachusetts, Michigan, Minnesota, Missouri, New Hampshire, New Jersey, Ohio, Oregon, Pennsylvania, Rhode Island, Vermont, West Virginia, and Wisconsin**.

19. The states that belonged to the Confederacy, or the South, were: **Alabama, Arkansas, Florida, Georgia, Louisiana, Mississippi, North Carolina, South Carolina, Tennessee, Texas, and Virginia**.

20. **Lincoln was shot** on April 15, 1865, one week after the Civil War ended, by a man who loved the South.

21. **The Union,** or **the North**, won the Civil War.

22. The "Star-Spangled Banner" is our **national anthem**, or song.

23. It was written by **Francis Scott Key**.

24. Francis Scott Key felt **very patriotic,** or **loyal**, to his country.

25. The first president was **George Washington**, the third president was **Thomas Jefferson**, and the sixteenth president was **Abraham Lincoln**.

Appendix 2

Commonly Asked Questions About U.S. Government

1. What is the highest law of the land?
2. What is the Constitution?
3. When was the Constitution adopted?
4. What is the form of government in the United States?
5. What is a democracy?
6. Can the Constitution be changed?
7. How many amendments does the Constitution have?
8. What is the Bill of Rights?
9. What are two of the rights guaranteed by the Bill of Rights?
10. What are some of the important amendments that are not in the Bill of Rights?
11. How many branches of government does the United States have? What are they?
12. What does the legislative branch do?
13. How many parts is Congress divided into? Name them.
14. How many members are there in the House of Representatives?
15. For how many years is a representative elected?
16. What is the name of your representative in Congress?
17. How many members are there in the Senate?
18. For how many years is a senator elected?
19. What are the names of your senators?
20. How many senators are elected from each state?
21. What does the judicial branch do?
22. What is the name of the highest court in the United States? How many judges (justices) are on this court?
23. Who picks the judges on this court?
24. How long can these judges serve?
25. Where is this court located?
26. What does the executive branch do?
27. Who is the leader of the executive branch?
28. Who is the president of the United States?
29. For how many years is a United States president elected?
30. How many times can a person be elected president of the United States?
31. What are the qualifications needed to be president of the United States?
32. Who takes the president's place if he cannot finish his time in office?
33. Who is the vice president of the United States?
34. What is the Cabinet?
35. How many presidents has the United States had to this date?

36. Can the president be removed from office? How?
37. How many states are in the United States?
38. What is the capital of the United States?
39. What are three basic requirements that allow a person to vote?
40. What are the two major political parties in the United States?
41. What political party does President Bush belong to?
42. Describe the American flag today.
43. What colors are on the American flag?
44. Describe the first American flag.
45. What legal holiday is February 12?
46. What legal holiday is July 4?
47. What legal holiday is November 11?
48. Who is the governor of your state?
49. Where is your state capital?
50. Who is the mayor of your city or town?

Answers to Questions About U.S. Government

1. The **Constitution** is the highest law of the land.

2. The Constitution is **a legal document that tells the rights of the citizens and the powers of the federal government.**

3. The Constitution was adopted in **1789.**

4. The form of government in the United States is called a **democracy**, or a **representative democracy.**

5. A democracy is a government in which the **people are governed by leaders whom they have elected.**

6. Changes can be made in the Constitution by **amendments.**

7. The Constitution now has **26** amendments. This includes the Bill of Rights.

8. The Bill of Rights is the **first 10 amendments** to the Constitution.

9. Some of the rights guaranteed by the Bill of Rights are: **freedom of speech, freedom of the press, freedom of religion, the right to peaceful assembly,** and **the right to a fair trial.**

10. Some other important amendments are:

    a. 13th: **no more slavery**

    b. 19th: **women can vote**

    c. 22nd: **the president can only be elected twice**

    d. 26th: **lowered the minimum voting age to 18**

11. The United States government has **three branches**. They are the **legislative, judicial, and executive**.

12. The legislative branch **makes the laws**.

13. Congress is divided into **two parts**. They are the **Senate** and the **House of Representatives**.

14. There are **435 members** in the House of Representatives.

15. A representative is elected for a **two-year term**.

16. The name of my representative is (answers will vary).

17. There are **100** members in the Senate.

18. A senator is elected for a **six-year term**.

19. My two senators are (answers will vary).

20. **Two senators** are elected from each state.

21. The judicial branch **interprets the laws**, or says what they mean.

22. The **Supreme Court** is the highest court in the United States. There are **nine judges** (justices) on the Supreme Court.

23. The **president** picks the Supreme Court judges.

24. These judges can serve **for life**.

25. The Supreme Court is in **Washington, D.C.**

26. The executive branch **enforces the laws**.

27. The **president** is the leader of the executive branch.

28. The president of the United States is **George Bush**.

29. The president of the United States is elected for a **four-year term**.

30. A person can be elected president of the United States **two times**.

31. To be president of the United States, you must be at least **35 years old, a 14-year resident of the United States, and born in the United States**.

32. The **vice president** would take the president's place.

33. The vice president of the United States is **Dan Quayle**.

34. The Cabinet is **14 secretaries of different departments** picked by the president to help him make decisions.

35. The United States has had **41 presidents**.

36. **Yes**, the president can be removed from office. He can be removed by **impeachment, trial, and conviction**.

37. There are **fifty states** in the United States.

38. **Washington, D.C.**, is the capital of the United States.

39. A person must be at least **18 years old, a citizen of the United States**, and **registered to vote** in his or her state at least 30 days before the election.

40. The two major political parties in the United States are the **Democratic Party** and the **Republican Party**.

41. President Bush belongs to the **Republican Party**.

42. The American flag has **13 red-and-white stripes and 50 white stars on a blue background**.

43. The colors on the American flag are **red, white, and blue**.

44. The first American flag had **13 red-and-white stripes and 13 white stars on a blue background**.

45. **Lincoln's Birthday** is the holiday on February 12.

46. July 4 is **Independence Day**, or the nation's birthday.

47. November 11 is called **Veterans Day**. It honors the men and women who served in the military.

48. The governor of my state is (answers will vary).

49. The state capital is (answers will vary).

50. The mayor is (answers will vary).

Appendix 3

Map of the United States

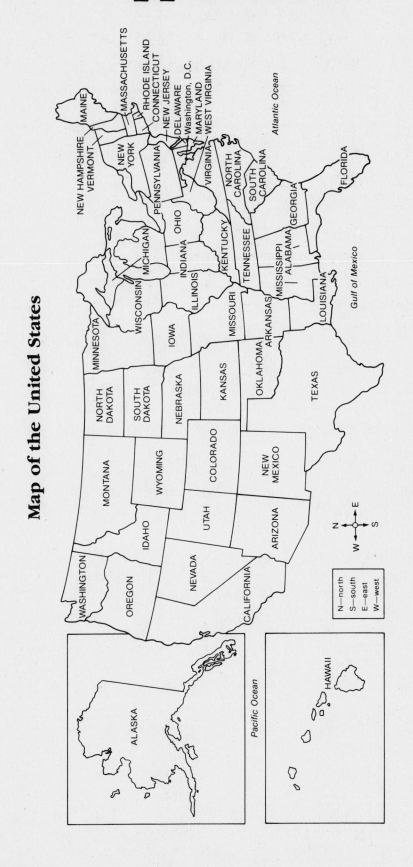

Appendix 4

The States and Their Capitals

State	Abbreviation	Capital
Alabama	AL	Montgomery
Alaska	AK	Juneau
Arizona	AZ	Phoenix
Arkansas	AR	Little Rock
California	CA	Sacramento
Colorado	CO	Denver
Connecticut	CT	Hartford
Delaware	DE	Dover
Florida	FL	Tallahassee
Georgia	GA	Atlanta
Hawaii	HI	Honolulu
Idaho	ID	Boise
Illinois	IL	Springfield
Indiana	IN	Indianapolis
Iowa	IA	Des Moines
Kansas	KS	Topeka
Kentucky	KY	Frankfort
Louisiana	LA	Baton Rouge
Maine	ME	Augusta
Maryland	MD	Annapolis
Massachusetts	MA	Boston
Michigan	MI	Lansing
Minnesota	MN	St. Paul
Mississippi	MS	Jackson

State	Abbreviation	Capital
Missouri	MO	Jefferson City
Montana	MT	Helena
Nebraska	NE	Lincoln
Nevada	NV	Carson City
New Hampshire	NH	Concord
New Jersey	NJ	Trenton
New Mexico	NM	Santa Fe
New York	NY	Albany
North Carolina	NC	Raleigh
North Dakota	ND	Bismarck
Ohio	OH	Columbus
Oklahoma	OK	Oklahoma City
Oregon	OR	Salem
Pennsylvania	PA	Harrisburg
Rhode Island	RI	Providence
South Carolina	SC	Columbia
South Dakota	SD	Pierre
Tennessee	TN	Nashville
Texas	TX	Austin
Utah	UT	Salt Lake City
Vermont	VT	Montpelier
Virginia	VA	Richmond
Washington	WA	Olympia
West Virginia	WV	Charleston
Wisconsin	WI	Madison
Wyoming	WY	Cheyenne

Appendix 5

1989

Months

January

February

March

April

May

June

July

August

September

October

November

December

Days of the Week

Sunday (Su)

Monday (M)

Tuesday (Tu)

Wednesday (W)

Thursday (Th)

Friday (F)

Saturday (Sa)

	S	M	T	W	T	F	S
JAN.	1	2	3	4	5	6	7
	8	9	10	11	12	13	14
	15	16	17	18	19	20	21
	22	23	24	25	26	27	28
	29	30	31				

FEB.			1	2	3	4
5	6	7	8	9	10	11
12	13	14	15	16	17	18
19	20	21	22	23	24	25
26	27	28				

MAR.			1	2	3	4
5	6	7	8	9	10	11
12	13	14	15	16	17	18
19	20	21	22	23	24	25
26	27	28	29	30	31	

APR.						1
2	3	4	5	6	7	8
9	10	11	12	13	14	15
16	17	18	19	20	21	22
23	24	25	26	27	28	29
30						

MAY		1	2	3	4	5	6
7	8	9	10	11	12	13
14	15	16	17	18	19	20
21	22	23	24	25	26	27
28	29	30	31			

JUNE				1	2	3
4	5	6	7	8	9	10
11	12	13	14	15	16	17
18	19	20	21	22	23	24
25	26	27	28	29	30	

JULY						1
2	3	4	5	6	7	8
9	10	11	12	13	14	15
16	17	18	19	20	21	22
23	24	25	26	27	28	29
30	31					

AUG.		1	2	3	4	5
6	7	8	9	10	11	12
13	14	15	16	17	18	19
20	21	22	23	24	25	26
27	28	29	30	31		

SEPT.					1	2
3	4	5	6	7	8	9
10	11	12	13	14	15	16
17	18	19	20	21	22	23
24	25	26	27	28	29	30

OCT.	1	2	3	4	5	6	7
8	9	10	11	12	13	14
15	16	17	18	19	20	21
22	23	24	25	26	27	28
29	30	31				

NOV.			1	2	3	4
5	6	7	8	9	10	11
12	13	14	15	16	17	18
19	20	21	22	23	24	25
26	27	28	29	30		

DEC.					1	2
3	4	5	6	7	8	9
10	11	12	13	14	15	16
17	18	19	20	21	22	23
24	25	26	27	28	29	30
31						

Holidays

New Year's Day—January 1

Martin Luther King, Jr., Day—January 16*
(Third Monday in January)

Lincoln's Birthday—February 12

Washington's Birthday—February 22

Memorial Day—May 29*
(Last Monday in May)

Fourth of July/Independence Day—July 4

Labor Day—September 4*
(First Monday in September)

Columbus Day—October 9*
(Second Monday in October)

Thanksgiving—November 23*
(Last Thursday in November)

Christmas—December 25

*These dates are different from year to year.

Appendix 6

United States Presidents (and years served)

1. George Washington (1789–1797)
2. John Adams (1797–1801)
3. Thomas Jefferson (1801–1809)
4. James Madison (1809–1817)
5. James Monroe (1817–1825)
6. John Q. Adams (1825–1829)
7. Andrew Jackson (1829–1837)
8. Martin Van Buren (1837–1841)
9. William Harrison (1841)
10. John Tyler (1841–1845)
11. James Polk (1845–1849)
12. Zachary Taylor (1849–1850)
13. Millard Fillmore (1850–1853)
14. Franklin Pierce (1853–1857)
15. James Buchanan (1857–1861)
16. Abraham Lincoln (1861–1865)
17. Andrew Johnson (1865–1869)
18. Ulysses Grant (1869–1877)
19. Rutherford Hayes (1877–1881)
20. James Garfield (1881)
21. Chester Arthur (1881–1885)
22. Grover Cleveland (1885–1889)
23. Benjamin Harrison (1889–1893)
24. Grover Cleveland (1893–1897)
25. William McKinley (1897–1901)
26. Theodore Roosevelt (1901–1909)
27. William Taft (1909–1913)
28. Woodrow Wilson (1913–1921)
29. Warren Harding (1921–1923)
30. Calvin Coolidge (1923–1929)
31. Herbert Hoover (1929–1933)
32. Franklin Roosevelt (1933–1945)
33. Harry Truman (1945–1953)
34. Dwight Eisenhower (1953–1961)
35. John Kennedy (1961–1963)
36. Lyndon Johnson (1963–1969)
37. Richard Nixon (1969–1974)
38. Gerald Ford (1974–1977)
39. Jimmy Carter (1977–1981)
40. Ronald Reagan (1981–1989)
41. George Bush (1989–   )

Answer Key

CHAPTER 1
NATIVE AMERICANS
After You Read
1. c
2. b
3. d
4. c

Using New Words
1. The first **inhabitants** of North America came from Asia.
2. The Native Americans developed a wide variety of **cultures** and languages.
3. A tragic **conflict** developed between the Europeans and the Native Americans.
4. The European colonists **abused** the Native Americans.
5. Native Americans have made many **contributions** to modern society, such as art and different crops.

Think About the Native Americans
Exact answers will vary.
1. The Native Americans originally came from Asia.
2. The first Native Americans crossed a small piece of land to enter North America from Asia.
3. The Native Americans lived in all parts of North and South America.
4. The Native Americans lived in many areas, and each area developed its own language.
5. The Europeans were able to dominate the Native Americans by using guns. They fought the Native Americans and took away their land.

CHAPTER 2
CHRISTOPHER COLUMBUS AND THE NEW WORLD
After You Read
1. d
2. b
3. c
4. b

Using New Words
1. A person who directs a sailing ship: **navigator**
2. The opposite of round: **flat**
3. To create communities in a new place: **colonize**

Think About Columbus
Exact answers will vary.
1. At the time of Columbus, Europeans traveled to Asia by land.
2. Columbus wanted to sail to Asia.
3. The Queen of Spain was wealthy and powerful.
4. Columbus thought he was sailing to Asia. India is a large Asian country.
5. After Columbus discovered the New World, Europeans began to come to live there.

CHAPTER 3
JAMESTOWN AND PLYMOUTH
After You Read
1. c
2. c
3. a
4. a

Using New Words
1. People left Europe to create **colonies** in North America.
2. At Plymouth, the Pilgrims **suffered** from sickness.
3. With help from the Indians, the Pilgrims had a good **harvest**.
4. After the first harvest, the Pilgrims celebrated with a great **meal**.

5. Families often have large get-togethers called **reunions** on Thanksgiving Day.

Think About Jamestown and Plymouth

Exact answers will vary.
1. Jamestown was the first permanent English colony in North America.
2. The Pilgrims suffered greatly from sickness and lack of food.
3. They were thankful for the good harvest.
4. On Thanksgiving Day we give thanks for our food and health just as the Pilgrims did.
5. Some of them wanted to be free to practice their religion.

CHAPTER 4
BEGINNINGS OF THE REVOLUTION
After You Read
1. a   3. d
2. c   4. d

Using New Words
1. Money paid to a government: **taxes**
2. People who fight for a country: **soldiers**
3. Power: **strength**
4. People who created the colonies: **colonists**
5. Guns and knives: **weapons**
6. Without weapons: **unarmed**

Think About Rebellion in the Colonies

Exact answers will vary.
1. The colonies were becoming stronger economically, and their population was growing.
2. The Boston Massacre began when colonists protested at the Customs House in Boston.
3. The colonists dressed like Indians so no one would know them.

4. The English government was angry about the Boston Tea Party because the colonists were disobeying the English and because the tea they destroyed was valuable.
5. The Boston Massacre and the Boston Tea Party were important because they were examples of the colonists' desire to be independent.

CHAPTER 5
THE DECLARATION OF INDEPENDENCE
After You Read
1. d   3. d
2. b   4. b

Using New Words
1. The colonies wanted to control themselves. They wanted **independence** from England.
2. The colonies showed England that they wanted more rights by **approving** the Declaration of Independence.
3. The rights of people are **proclaimed** by the Declaration of Independence.
4. The day that the Declaration of Independence was approved is known as the **birthday** of the United States.

Think About the Declaration of Independence

Exact answers will vary.
1. The colonists wanted to write a formal explanation of why they wanted to be independent.
2. The colonists wanted to have control over themselves.
3. The Declaration of Independence was approved on July 4, 1776.
4. It was important that representatives of all the colonies signed the Declaration of Independence because this showed that the colonies were united in their desire for independence.

5. The King of England was not happy with the Declaration of Independence because he did not want to lose control of the colonies.

CHAPTER 6
GEORGE WASHINGTON AND THE REVOLUTION
After You Read

1. d   3. a
2. a   4. c

Using New Words

1. Members of an army: **soldiers**
2. The army or country you fight against: **enemy**
3. Gave up: **surrendered**
4. The leader of the American government: **president**

Think About the American Revolution

Exact answers will vary.
1. The Revolutionary War began in 1775. It ended in 1783.
2. Paul Revere told the colonists that the English were coming.
3. As a result of the Revolutionary War, the colonies became independent.
4. The colonists had to fight for independence because the English did not want to lose control of the colonies.
5. George Washington is famous because he was an important leader of the colonists in the fight for independence and was the first president of the United States.

CHAPTER REVIEW 1
Word Find

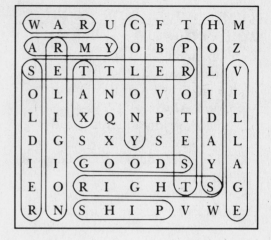

Timeline

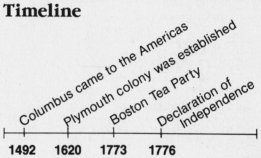

Map Activity
Check your answers against the map on page 21.

Quiz

1. Christopher Columbus was a European who found the New World in 1492.
2. The first English settlements were in Jamestown, Virginia, and in Plymouth, Massachusetts.
3. The people who settled Plymouth were called Pilgrims. They wanted religious freedom in the New World.
4. In 1773, colonists protested a tax on tea. They went to ships in Boston Harbor and threw the tea into the water.
5. There were 13 English colonies.
6. Thomas Jefferson wrote most of the Declaration of Independence.
7. The birthdate is the Fourth of July, or Independence Day.

8. The Revolutionary War is the war in which the U.S. won independence from England.
9. The great leader of this war was George Washington.
10. The first president of the U.S. was George Washington.

CHAPTER 7
THE BIRTH OF THE CONSTITUTION
After You Read
1. d
2. a
3. c
4. c

Using New Words
1. Acceptable; good: **satisfactory**
2. The opposite of strong: **weak**
3. To make someone do something: to **force**
4. Rules: **laws**
5. Form; shape: **structure**

Think About the Continental Congress and the Constitution
Exact answers will vary.
1. An important problem with the Articles of Confederation was that they did not give enough power to the federal government.
2. The Constitution replaced the Articles of Confederation.
3. Documents like the Articles of Confederation and the Constitution are important because they clearly explain who has power in a government.
4. It was important that every state approved the Constitution because this showed that all states were going to obey the Constitution.
5. The Constitution is an important document because it contains the most important laws of the United States.

CHAPTER 8
THE AMERICAN FLAG
After You Read
1. b
2. c
3. c
4. c

Using New Words
1. There are 13 of these on the American flag: **stripes**
2. There are 50 of these on the American flag: **stars**
3. new; recent: **modern**
4. to show that you care about something: to show **respect**

Think About the American Flag
Exact answers will vary.
1. There are 50 stars on the flag to represent the 50 states.
2. There are 13 stripes on the flag to represent the 13 original colonies.
3. The flag is a symbol of the U.S. government.
4. Americans put out flags on the Fourth of July to show respect for their country.
5. Answers will vary.

CHAPTER 9
THE WAR OF 1812 AND THE "STAR-SPANGLED BANNER"
After You Read
1. b
2. d
3. c
4. b

Using New Words
1. Continued or went on: **progressed**
2. Watched: **observed**
3. A fight or struggle in a war: **battle**
4. A symbol of a country: **flag**
5. The national song of a country: **anthem**

Think About the War of 1812

Exact answers will vary.

1. The United States was angry with England because the English were taking Americans from American ships.
2. The English took their citizens from American ships because they needed soldiers in the war against France.
3. During the War of 1812 the English set fire to the White House.
4. Francis Scott Key was inspired when he saw the American flag still flying after a difficult battle.
5. The United States fought against England in the Revolutionary War and the War of 1812.

CHAPTER 10 ABRAHAM LINCOLN AND THE CIVIL WAR

After You Read

1. a   3. b
2. d   4. d

Using New Words

1. The **economy** of the South was based on farming.
2. Today, people can't be bought and sold in the U.S. **Slavery** is illegal.
3. Slaves were **descendants** of people from Africa because they were their children, grandchildren, and great-grandchildren.
4. Slaves were thought of as **property**, just like land.
5. Many Northerners **opposed** slavery because it's wrong.

Think About the Civil War

Exact answers will vary.

1. The economy of the South was based on slavery; the economy of the North was not.
2. Lincoln was assassinated while he was president.
3. Lincoln is considered to be a great president because he kept the United States together and he helped to end slavery.
4. Slavery was good for the economy of the South.
5. The factories in the North could produce manufactured goods like guns.

CHAPTER 11 EXPANSION AND IMMIGRATION

After You Read

1. c   3. b
2. d   4. a

Using New Words

1. Reached from one place to another: **extended**
2. To make bigger or better: **develop**
3. People who go to live in another country: **immigrants**
4. A growth or increase in size: **expansion**

Think About the Expansion of the United States

Exact answers will vary.

1. The Louisiana Purchase included territory west of the Mississippi River to the Rocky Mountains, and south from Canada to the Gulf of Mexico.
2. After a war with Mexico, the United States took possession of territory between the Rocky Mountains and the Pacific Ocean.
3. Today, immigrants to the U.S. come from many countries. The examples in the passage were Vietnam, the Philippines, and Mexico.
4. Many immigrants come to find jobs, or they come for political reasons.
5. Many immigrants came to find jobs, land, and freedom.

CHAPTER 12
THE UNITED STATES IN THE WORLD WARS
After You Read

1. d	**3.** a
2. a	**4.** d

Using New Words

1. The United States didn't want to take sides in the war; it wanted to stay **neutral**.
2. U.S. ships were bombed at the **naval** base called Pearl Harbor.
3. The **atomic bomb** can kill thousands of people at a time.
4. The United States created, or **invented**, the atomic bomb.
5. American products and music have had a great **influence** on the rest of the world.

Think About the World Wars

Exact answers will vary.
1. The United States entered World War I in 1917.
2. In World War II, the United States fought against Japan, Germany, and Italy.
3. The United States used the atomic bomb against Japan.
4. They had to produce goods for the war, like guns and airplanes.
5. Some other countries became less powerful as the United States gained influence.

CHAPTER REVIEW 2
Word Find

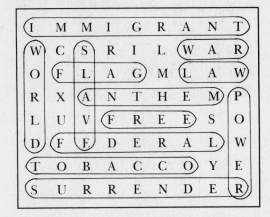

Timeline

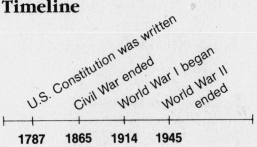

Map Activity

Check your answers against the map on page 47.

Quiz

1. The Constitution is the supreme law of the land. It defines the structure and powers of the federal government.
2. The Constitution was adopted in 1789.
3. The "Star-Spangled Banner" is our national song, or anthem.
4. It was written by Francis Scott Key.
5. It was a war between the North and the South to free the slaves.
6. Abraham Lincoln was president during the Civil War.
7. The Union (the North) won the Civil War.
8. Lincoln was killed after the Civil War ended.
9. Immigrants came to have land and get jobs.
10. The U.S. entered World War II because Japan bombed Pearl Harbor.

CHAPTER 13
WHAT IS DEMOCRACY?
After You Read

1. a   3. c
2. d   4. c

Using New Words

1. Citizens have the **right** to believe in any religion.
2. Representatives should **protect** people's rights.
3. **Democracy** is a type of government.
4. In a democracy, the **government** is controlled by the people.
5. Citizens **elect** representatives in the United States.

Think About Democracy

Exact answers will vary.

1. Democracy is a type of government in which citizens are the final authority.
2. Citizens choose representatives in elections.
3. Some of the important rights described in the Constitution include the right to freedom of speech, the right to practice any religion, and the right to own property. Also, the Constitution says that people cannot be put in jail without a fair trial.
4. Elections are important because they allow citizens to change the government.
5. It is important for citizens to vote so they can express their views.

CHAPTER 14
THE U.S. CONSTITUTION
After You Read

1. d   3. b
2. b   4. a

Using New Words

1. In 1789, the **original** Constitution was adopted.
2. The Constitution created three **branches** of government.
3. Each area of the government has its own **responsibilities**.
4. Courts and **judges** are part of the judicial branch.
5. The Bill of Rights **guarantees** certain rights to the people.
6. The Bill of Rights consists of 10 **amendments** to the Constitution.

Think About the U.S. Constitution

Exact answers will vary.

1. The Constitution is a description of how the American government functions.
2. The Constitution created three branches of government in order to divide power.
3. The three branches of government are the executive, the legislative, and the judicial branches.
4. The Constitution makes the American government stable because it divides power among different areas of government.
5. The Constitution has been amended in order to change as American society changes.

CHAPTER 15
THREE BRANCHES OF U.S. GOVERNMENT
After You Read

1. d   3. a
2. c   4. d

Using New Words

1. This branch of government includes the Congress: **legislative branch**
2. This branch of government includes the court system: **judicial branch**
3. Not allowed by the Constitution: **unconstitutional**
4. To work together: **interact**

Think About the Three Branches of Government

Exact answers will vary.

1. Power is divided among the three branches of government so that no

one area of government is too powerful.
2. The legislative branch of government creates laws.
3. The judicial branch punishes lawbreakers.
4. The judicial branch decides if a law is permitted by the Constitution.
5. The Department of Transportation is used to make sure laws are obeyed. It is controlled by the executive branch.

CHAPTER 16
THE EXECUTIVE BRANCH
After You Read
1. d   3. c
2. d   4. a

Using New Words
1. The president lives in this building: **White House**
2. To make sure about something: **verify**
3. The army, navy, and air force are members of this group: **military**
4. A responsibility or an obligation: **duty**
5. This occurs when the number of "yes" and "no" votes is the same: **tie**

Think About the Executive Branch
Exact answers will vary.
1. Three important divisions of the executive branch are the president, the vice president, and the president's cabinet.
2. The president verifies that the laws of the nation are obeyed. He is also the commander in chief of the military.
3. The vice president can take the place of the president if the president cannot serve. He also can vote in the Senate.

4. The president meets with the members of the cabinet to learn about their activities and to get advice.
5. The number of years that a person can be president is limited so that one person does not become too powerful.

CHAPTER 17
THE LEGISLATIVE BRANCH
After You Read
1. a   3. c
2. d   4. c

Using New Words
1. A problem was **solved** by the creation of two houses of Congress.
2. Congress sends **bills** to the president for approval.
3. The **term** of a senator is six years.
4. The president can **veto** a bill.
5. Since many people live in California, the state is known for its large **population**.

Think About the Legislative Branch
Exact answers will vary.
1. There are two houses of Congress. These houses are the House of Representatives and the Senate.
2. The two houses of Congress have different numbers of members. The two houses are different because they represent the states in different ways.
3. The number of representatives that a state has depends on the population of that state. California has more representatives than Nevada because California has a larger population.
4. The term of a senator is six years.
5. The term of a representative is two years.

CHAPTER 18
THE JUDICIAL BRANCH
After You Read
1. d   3. c
2. b   4. a

Using New Words
1. These are interpreted in the courts: **laws**
2. The person in charge of a court: **judge**
3. The title of the Supreme Court judges: **justices**
4. More than half: **majority**
5. Way of thinking: **philosophy**

Think About the Judicial Branch
Exact answers will vary.
1. Supreme Court justices are chosen by the president and approved by the Senate.
2. The Supreme Court justices make decisions by voting.
3. The Supreme Court is the most important court because it can change the decisions of lower courts.
4. Answers will vary. A possible answer is so that the Supreme Court will have stability.
5. Answers will vary. A possible reason is that Washington, D.C., is the U.S. capital.

CHAPTER REVIEW 3
Word Find

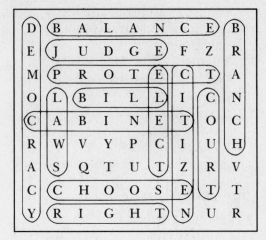

Find Out
Your teacher can give you the correct answers.

Match-up
Executive
1. runs the military
2. makes sure laws are obeyed
3. includes the cabinet

Legislative
1. writes new laws
2. has senators and representatives
3. has two parts, or houses

Judicial
1. punishes people who break the law
2. explains the laws
3. makes sure that laws agree with the Constitution

Quiz
1. The form of government in the U.S. is called a democracy, or a representative democracy.
2. There are three branches of government: legislative, executive, and judicial.
3. The legislative branch makes the laws.
   The executive branch makes sure laws are obeyed.
   The judicial branch interprets the laws.

116

4. The two parts of Congress are the House of Representatives and the Senate.
5. There are 435 members in the House of Representatives.
6. The term of office for a representative is two years.
7. There are 100 members in the Senate.
8. The term of office for a senator is six years.
9. The term of office for a president is four years.
10. If the president cannot finish his term, the vice president takes his place.
11. A president can be elected twice.
12. The highest court in the land is the Supreme Court.
13. The president picks the judges on this court.
14. Judges on the Supreme Court can serve for life.
15. The Supreme Court is located in Washington, D.C.

CHAPTER 19
THE BILL OF RIGHTS
After You Read
1. c
3. b
2. c
4. a

Using New Words
1. A person has the right to a fair **trial** in court.
2. The Constitution can be **changed** by the use of amendments.
3. The Bill of Rights says that the government cannot be **cruel** to a person.
4. The Bill of Rights places **restrictions** on the government.
5. A person accused of a crime has a right to be defended by a **lawyer**.

Think About the Bill of Rights
Exact answers will vary.
1. The Bill of Rights was added to the Constitution in 1791.

2. The Bill of Rights consists of 10 amendments to the Constitution. These amendments protect the rights of people and limit the power of the government.
3. Two kinds of protection provided by the Bill of Rights are the right to freedom of speech and the right to freedom of religion.
4. Answers will vary. A possible answer is that people should be able to believe whatever they want to.
5. Answers will vary. A possible answer is that people have a right to their own privacy.

CHAPTER 20
OTHER AMENDMENTS TO THE CONSTITUTION
After You Read
1. c
3. c
2. b
4. b

Using New Words
1. People of any race are **allowed** to vote.
2. The Constitution is **flexible** and can be changed.
3. It is **illegal** to have slaves in the United States.
4. To get money, the government can **tax** the citizens.
5. Some amendments help the government **function** better.

Think About the Amendments to the Constitution
Exact answers will vary.
1. There are 26 amendments to the Constitution.
2. The 15th, 19th, 24th, and 26th amendments make it easier for people to vote.
3. The 16th Amendment provided the government with more money.
4. Two-thirds of each house of Congress must approve the amendment, and three-fourths of the states must approve it also.

5. Before the 24th Amendment, some people could not vote because they could not afford to pay to vote.

CHAPTER 21
THE VOTING PROCESS
After You Read
1. d   3. a
2. d   4. d

Using New Words
1. People vote for **candidates** in an election.
2. There are two major political **parties** in the United States.
3. Citizens must be **registered** before they can vote.
4. A **voter** must be at least 18 years old.
5. A person's vote is a **secret**.

Think About Voting and Elections
Exact answers will vary.
1. The two largest political parties are the Democratic Party and the Republican Party.
2. Any citizen over the age of 18 who is registered can vote.
3. Amendments about voting were added in order to allow more people to vote.
4. Answers will vary. One possible answer is that when they register, people must give evidence that they live in the area.
5. Answers will vary. One possible answer is that people should be encouraged but not required to vote.

CHAPTER REVIEW 4
Word Find

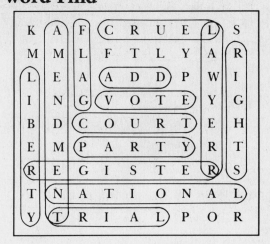

Match-up
1. c   3. g   5. e   7. b
2. d   4. h   6. f   8. a

Quiz
1. Yes, the Constitution can be changed by an amendment.
2. The Constitution has 26 amendments.
3. The Bill of Rights is the first 10 amendments to the Constitution.
4. Some of the rights guaranteed by the Bill of Rights are freedom of speech, freedom of religion, freedom of the press, and the right to a fair trial.
5. Some other important amendments are:
   13th: no more slavery
   19th: women can vote
   22nd: a person can only be elected president twice
   26th: lowered minimum voting age to 18
6. To vote you must be at least 18, a citizen of the U.S., live in your state a certain period of time, and be registered to vote.
7. The two major political parties are the Republican Party and the Democratic Party.

U.S. Department of Justice
Immigration and Naturalization Service

Application to Adjust Status from Temporary to Permanent Resident
(Under Section 245 A of Public Law 99-603)

Please read instructions: fee will not be refunded.	Fee Stamp
INS Use: Bar Code SAMPLE	
Address Label	
(Place adhesive address label here from booklet **or** fill in name and address, and A 90 million file number in appropriate blocks.)	Applicant's File No. A - 9 _ _ _ _ _ _ _

1. Family Name *(Last Name in CAPITAL Letters) (See instructions) (First Name) (Middle Name)*

2. Sex ☐ Male ☐ Female

3. Name as it appears on Temporary Resident Card *(I-688)* if different from above.

4. Phone No.'s *(Include Area Codes)*
Home:
Work:

5. Reason for difference in name *(See instructions)*

6. Home Address *(No. and Street)*   *(Apt. No.)*   *(City)*   *(State)*   *(Zip Code)*

7. Mailing Address *(if different)*   *(Apt. No.)*   *(City)*   *(State)*   *(Zip Code)*

8. Place of Birth *(City or Town)*   *(County, Province or State) (Country)*

9. Date of Birth *(Month/Day/Year)*

10. Your Mother's First Name

11. Your Father's First Name

12. Enter your Social Security Number
_ _ _ - _ _ - _ _ _ _

13. Absences from the United States since becoming a Temporary Resident Alien. *(List most recent first.) (If you have a single absence in excess of 30 days or the total of all your absences exceeds 90 days, explain and attach any relevant information).*

Country	Purpose of Trip	From (Month/Day/Year)	To (Month/Day/Year)	Total Days Absent

14. When applying for temporary resident alien status, I
☐ did ☐ did not submit a medical examination form (I-693) with my application that included a serologic (blood) test for human immunodeficiency virus (HIV) infection. *(If you did not, submit a medical examination form (I-693) with this application that includes a serologic test for HIV.)*

15. Since becoming a temporary resident alien, I
☐ have ☐ have not been arrested, convicted or confined in a prison. *(If you have, provide the date(s), place(s), specific charge(s) and attach any relevant information.)*

16. Since becoming a temporary resident alien, I
☐ have ☐ have not been the beneficiary of a pardon, amnesty (other than legalization), rehabilitation decree, other act of clemency or similar action. *(If you have, explain and attach any relevant documentation.)*

17. Since becoming a temporary resident alien, I
☐ have ☐ have not received public assistance from any source, including but not limited to, the United States Government, any state, county, city or municipality. *(If you have, explain, including the name(s) and Social Security Number(s) used and attach any relevant information.)*

Form I-698 (08/10/88) Page 1

18. Concerning the requirement of minimal understanding of ordinary English and a knowledge and understanding of the history and government of the United States: *(Check appropriate block under Section A or B.)*

A. I will satisfy these requirements by;
☐ Examination at the time of interview for permanent residence.
☐ Satisfactorily pursuing a course of study recognized by the Attorney General.

B. I have satisfied these requirements by;
☐ Having satisfactorily pursued a course of study recognized by the Attorney General *(please attach appropriate documentation).*
☐ Exemption, in that I am 65 years of age or older, under the age of 16, or I am physically unable to comply. *(If physically unable to comply, explain and attach relevant documentation.)*

19. Applicants for status as Permanent Residents must establish that they are not excludable from the United States under the following provisions of section 212 of the INA. An applicant who is excludable under a provision of section 212 (a) which may not be waived is ineligible for permanent resident status. An applicant who is excludable under a provision of section 212 (a) which may be waived may, if otherwise eligible, be granted permanent resident status, if an application for waiver on form I-690 is filed and approved.

A. Grounds for exclusion which *may not be waived:*
● Listed by paragraph number of section 212 (a);
____ (9) Aliens who have committed or who have been convicted of a crime involving moral turpitude (does not include minor traffic violations).
____ (10) Aliens who have been convicted of two or more offenses for which the aggregate sentences to confinement actually imposed were five years or more.
____ (15) Aliens likely to become a public charge.
____ (23) Aliens who have been convicted of a violation of any law or regulation relating to narcotic drugs or marihuana, or who have been illicit traffickers in narcotic drugs or marihuana.
____ (27) Aliens who intend to engage in activities prejudicial to the national interests or unlawful activities of a subversive nature.
____ (28) Aliens who are or at any time have been anarchists, or members of or affiliated with any Communist or other totalitarian party, including any subdivision or affiliate thereof.
____ (29) Aliens who have advocated or taught, either by personal utterance, or by means of any written matter, or through affiliation with an organization:
1) Opposition to organized government;
2) The overthrow of government by force or violence;
3) The assaulting or killing of government officials because of their official character;
4) The unlawful destruction of property;
5) Sabotage, or;
6) The doctrines of world communism, or the establishment of a totalitarian dictatorship in the United States.
____ (33) Aliens who, during the period beginning on March 23, 1933, and ending on May 8, 1945, under the direction of, and in association with:
1) The Nazi government in Germany;
2) Any government in any area occupied by the military forces of the Nazi government in Germany;
3) Any government established with the assistance or cooperation of the Nazi government of Germany;
4) Any government which was an ally of the Nazi government of Germany;
ordered, incited, assisted or otherwise participated in the persecution of any person because of race, religion, national origin, or political opinion.
● Provisions of 212 (e):
____ Aliens who at any time were exchange visitors subject to the two-year foreign residence requirement unless the requirement has been satisfied or waived pursuant to the provisions of section 212 (e) of the Act. (Does not apply to the Extended Voluntary Departure (EVD) class of temporary resident aliens).

B. Grounds for exclusion which *may be waived:*
● Listed by paragraph number of section 212 (a);
____ (1) Aliens who are mentally retarded.
____ (2) Aliens who are insane.
____ (3) Aliens who have suffered one or more attacks of insanity.
____ (4) Aliens afflicted with psychopathic personality, sexual deviation, or a mental defect.
____ (5) Aliens who are narcotic drug addicts or chronic alcoholics.
____ (6) Aliens who are afflicted with any dangerous contagious disease.
____ (7) Aliens who have a physical defect, disease or disability affecting their ability to earn a living.
____ (8) Aliens who are paupers, professional beggars or vagrants.
____ (11) Aliens who are polygamists or advocate polygamy.
____ (12) Aliens who are prostitutes or former prostitutes, or who have procured or attempted to procure or to import, prostitutes or persons for the purpose of prostitution or for any other immoral purpose, or aliens coming to the United States to engage in any other unlawful commercialized vice, whether or not related to prostitution.
____ (13) Aliens coming to the United States to engage in any immoral sexual act.
____ (16) Aliens who have been excluded from admission and deported and who again seek admission within one year from the date of such deportation.
____ (17) Aliens who have been arrested and deported and who reentered the United States within five years from the date of deportation.
____ (19) Aliens who have procured or have attempted to procure a visa or other documentation by fraud, or by willfully misrepresenting a material fact.
____ (22) Aliens who have applied for exemption or discharge from training or service in the Armed Forces of the United States on the ground of alienage and who have been relieved or discharged from such training or service.
____ (31) Aliens who at any time shall have, knowingly and for gain, encouraged, induced, assisted, abetted, or aided any other alien to enter or to try to enter the United States in violation of law.

Do any of the above classes apply to you?
☐ No ☐ Yes *(If "Yes", attach an explanation, and any relevant documentation. Place mark (X) on line before ground(s) of exclusion.)*

Do any of the above classes apply to you?
☐ No ☐ Yes *(If "Yes", attach an explanation, and any relevant documentation and submit Form I-690. Place mark (X) on line before ground(s) of exclusion.)*

20. If your native alphabet is other than Roman letters, write your name in your native alphabet.	21. Language of native alphabet
22. Signature of Applicant - *I CERTIFY*, under penalty of perjury under the laws of the United States of America that the foregoing is true and correct. I hereby consent and authorize the Service to verify the information provided, and to conduct record checks pertinent to this application.	23. Date *(Month/Day/Year)*
24. Signature of person preparing form, if other than applicant. I DECLARE that this document was prepared by me at the request of the applicant and is based on all information of which I have any knowledge.	25. Date *(Month/Day/Year)*
26. Name and Address of person preparing form, **if other than applicant** *(type or print)*.	27. Occupation